THE
ENGLISH FACT
IN QUEBEC

Sheila McLeod Arnopoulos
Dominique Clift

THE ENGLISH FACT IN QUEBEC

**McGill-Queen's University Press
Montreal**

© McGill-Queen's University Press 1980

ISBN 0-7735-0358-7 (cloth)
ISBN 0-7735-0359-5 (paper)

Legal deposit first quarter 1980
Bibliothèque nationale du Québec

A French-language edition of this work has
been published by Libre Expression under
the title *Le Fait anglais au Québec*.

Cover photo: Patrice Puiberneau

Printed in Canada by Imprimerie Gagné Ltée

Contents

The French tendency to resort to isolation as a means of cultural defence is illustrated by the seigneurial system, the symbol of the rejection of English commercial culture at the beginning of the nineteenth century.

The type of capitalism existing in Canada at the beginning of the nineteenth century was the same as that which had brought on the American Revolution in 1776.

The English community recognizes only individual rights, an attitude which presupposes a homogeneous and English-speaking Canada. To this, the French oppose the notion of collective rights which is designed to assert their exclusive control over Quebec.

Although language has always been a source of conflict, it became a serious political issue only after religious and ethnic sentiments faded as collective rallying points, that is, after 1960.

The arbitration of English-French conflicts during the
first half of the twentieth century took place within the
Liberal party, and not in Parliament or in the cabinet. In
this respect, Canada resembles a one-party state.

The defence of the English school system against
nationalist attacks rests on the idea of a historical pact
between two nations whereby the economy was English
and society was French.

The rise of Quebec bureaucracy after 1960 ended the
autonomy of community institutions, thereby destroying
the power of the Catholic clergy and forcing the English
into the ambit of Quebec politics.

The opposition of Montreal's financial elite to the decentralization of the Canadian economy helped transform the
Quebec regionalism of the 1960s into the French
nationalism of the 1970s.

The unwillingness of the English-language press in
Quebec to discuss problems of integration stems from a
desire not to offend its public and from the absence of any
tradition of public debate within the English community.

Acknowledgements

This book owes a great deal to many persons to whom we wish to express our gratitude.

Professor Hubert Guindon of Concordia University, Professor Raymond Breton of the University of Toronto, Professor James Taylor of the Université de Montréal, and Elizabeth Van Every-Taylor have helped us define the topic we wished to approach.

Noël Pérusse, Sheila Fischman, and Margot Gibb-Clark, with their advice and criticism, have helped us bring our project to conclusion.

Special recognition is due to Mark Wilson for helping prepare the copy for English publication.

All great civilizations are basically cross-roads civilizations which have been able to harmonize in themselves influences of diverse origin. If this diversity were to disappear from an increasingly homogeneous and uniform world, there would be reason to fear that humanity was entering a period bearing little relationship to everything to which we traditionally have been attached.

Claude Lévi-Strauss

Introduction

The English fact in Quebec is the focal point of a crisis which is much broader in scope than Quebec and which has been draining the country's vitality and resources into an unproductive confrontation. This book, written in the form of essays, deals with a wide range of English-French encounters to explain how they have influenced the political and economic growth of Canada. The book also attempts to identify the changes in Canadian society that have caused a resurgence of English-French animosity in recent years.

The persistence of ethnic and cultural conflicts through the years indicates that Canada as a country has not yet realized a national identity. It also indicates that neither English Canada nor French Canada has attained the kind of collective maturity that makes it possible to accept the other into a national partnership. The booing of the French version of the national anthem that takes place when the Montreal Canadiens play in other Canadian cities, or the refusal of the other provinces to accept French school boards with independent taxing powers, speaks of a society that is unsure of its culture and of its goals. The same considerations apply to French Quebec's attempts to squeeze the English language out of public life. Indeed, both English and French are very much alike. Their respective intolerance tends to assume the same forms.

One obvious reason why the present confrontation or crisis overshadows those of the past is that Quebec has the economic and social capacity to secede and that it may, within a relatively short time, develop the collective will to do so. This introduces a new dimension in the historical rivalry between the two groups.

But it is not only French Quebec that has changed. English Montreal, which used to be the centre of what historian Donald Creighton called the Commercial Empire of the St. Lawrence, has lost its power and its leadership. The centre of economic activity has moved westwards. Having been deprived of its historical mission as managers of the national economy, Montreal's English community finds itself hard-pressed by the French middle class, which wants to be in sole control of the provincial and regional economy of Quebec. In these circumstances, it is difficult but certainly not impossible to maintain the English fact in Quebec, a phrase or concept modelled on its earlier counterpart, the French fact in Canada.

The decline of Montreal has coincided with the increasing balkanization of the Canadian economy. Regionalism is steadily gaining over the centralizing and integrative forces that have predominated throughout Canadian history. The regional division of labour or regional specialization, the semi-colonial relationship imposed on outlying areas by the centre, has been coming under severe attack, particularly from the Western provinces. Similarly, mass education and mass media have contributed to rising expectations. As a result, the ethnic stratification that has come to be known euphemistically as the Canadian Mosaic is slowly giving way to pluralism. Even though some of the old ethnic pecking order may survive, its social and ideological foundations have been crumbling. English Canada is now very different from what it was only a generation ago.

Even though these changes may be very desirable in themselves, they nevertheless constitute sources of great tension. True to their common history and to their very long association, English and French tend to blame each other for the disorientation they experience, which they cannot readily explain. One could say that there is something unhealthy in the way both groups have been acting as scapegoats for each other. Yet the transformations that are now taking place, unprecedented as they are here, may actually represent a sort of coming-of-age process.

For English Canada the process means that social values should no longer be subordinated to economic efficiency and expediency. It may generate the desire to end the economic, scientific, and cultural dependence on the United States, a relationship which has been eagerly accepted and which has only served to perpetuate the immaturity of Canadian society. For French Canada, the same process of coming of age may result in a greater capacity to see growth and independence in other terms than opposition to so-called English oppression.

Although it is hardly a centre of national power any more, Montreal can still continue to play an extremely important role in a country that is rapidly becoming regionalized and where power is increasingly fragmented. The city is no longer burdened with old economic structures and it can readily free itself from outmoded concepts of social and economic organization. Montreal possesses a cultural and linguistic diversity that often is the basis for innovation and far-reaching influence.

The city's future role, however, depends on the way English and French are able to come to terms with each other. Indeed, the manner in which the reconciliation is finally realized could very well exert a profound influence on the way the French look upon the rest of Canada and how they perceive their participation in Confederation or in any other arrangement that might take its place.

But this book does not offer any formula that might help resolve the issues that are at the root of current tensions and that are threatening the very existence of the country and the survival of the English community in Montreal. Nor does it offer any forecast as to how events will turn out. It only seeks to clarify the problems facing Canada.

The differences between this version and the French one published in October 1979 by Libre Expression are as follows: the introduction is entirely new, and the epilogue has been expanded to include a discussion of some specific issues concerning the English community and the ethnic minorities in Montreal. Some passages, explanatory in French but redundant in English, have been taken out and some new ones have been added where appropriate; they amount to relatively minor changes.

HISTORICAL PERSPECTIVES

Social Conflict and the Seigneurial System

The period in Quebec's history that best reflects the kind of tensions now dividing French and English is that preceding the Rebellion of 1837 and 1838. The resemblance has nothing to do with the violence and the armed insurrection that broke out at the time. It is that our period and that of the *Patriotes*, as the ultra-nationalists were then known, share a mental habit of casting every claim and every confrontation in ideological and ethnic terms. Intransigence is characteristic of both periods.

The kind of nationalism that is now associated with Quebec took shape in the early part of the nineteenth century. Of course, the French had long been conscious of forming a distinct religious and linguistic community: that feeling had already surfaced during the French colonial period of the seventeenth and eighteenth centuries. But it became much more pronounced under British rule, particularly as official policy kept swinging back and forth between the desire to submerge the French and Catholic population in an Anglo-Protestant majority and the need to recognize the permanence of French settlement in Lower Canada.

As the economy expanded and diversified, as social institutions cemented the bonds holding people together, the idea of a distinct and independent nationality gradually took hold among the French. The Constitutional Act of 1791 promoted political awareness by ineptly opposing the legislature to the executive authority of the governor and the advisers he chose for himself. This unusual constitutional system established a pattern of confrontation between the French legislature, preoccupied mainly with social organization and culture, and an English executive authority, concerned above all with commerce. As national awareness grew among the French, merchants such as James McGill and John Richardson helped consolidate the economic vocation of the English-speaking population.

It is during this same period that the views held by the French and the English about each other began to set. Stereotyped images of ethnic character, of national behaviour and attitudes, hardened to the point where they dominated political discussions and undercut any possibility of compromise and of adaptation to changing circumstances.

While recognizing that the French population was exceptionally industrious, the English commented upon its inclination for routine, lack of initiative, ineptness in business, absence of discipline, and general misunderstanding of the nature of progress. The English could not fathom the French attachment to archaic customs and institutions which no longer ensured well-being and which stood in the way of the country's prosperity. The French, on the other hand, looked down upon the English as materialistic, puritan, greedy, intrusive, and unsubtle. The English, they thought, were prone to impose their views and ways of doing things as standards towards which all others should strive. Each group, because of the prejudices it held about the other and the illusions it entertained about itself, gradually became so intransigent that public administration became paralysed, paving the way for the Rebellion of 1837.

The profound antagonism which came to the fore at the time went far beyond ethnic rivalry. As is the case today, the conflict was about the very organization of society and the goals of economic activity. It came to a head only at the beginning of the nineteenth century because until then French and English had been able to exist on the same territory and within the same political institutions without impinging too much on each other's interests. However, the demographic growth of the French and the material progress of the English made it imperative to harmonize interests that were diverging widely. This is precisely what Lower Canada was unable to achieve, or even to imagine, during this period when a final showdown seemed more and more inevitable.

The question which provoked the most profound and lasting animosity was the reform of the seigneurial system, a form of land tenure which France had imposed on the colony as a means of ensuring settlement and which the British had maintained along with all the customs and rights stemming from it.

English and American merchants who arrived in the colony after the Conquest in 1759 bitterly complained of having to submit to French laws and customs while under the authority of the British Crown. They attacked the system of land tenure as an unfortunate vestige from the Middle Ages and as a hindrance to commerce and to progress in general. The French population, on the other hand, believed the system to be essential for its cultural survival, all the more so as the opposition of the English merchant class grew steadily.

The conflict reflected a fundamental opposition between the organization of society as desired by the French and the organization of the economy as pursued by the English. The French elites believed that cultural security could be obtained by preserving an archaic legal system which made no provision for commercial activities and did not recognize the primacy of economics. English merchants, eager for commercial gain, acted as if social organization should be subordinated to economic pursuits. Accordingly they wanted to do away with the French system of land tenure and, at the same time, deal what could have been a mortal blow to the French society of Lower Canada. The defences went up to meet the threat. In this way the system of land tenure and of law became a sort of shell or armour against the English capitalist invasion.

The social system established in New France and which survived under British rule was not really an accidental survival from feudal days, though it retained many characteristics of that period. It is important to remember that as early as the sixteenth and seventeenth centuries France had a highly centralized government which foreshadowed the modern state with its fussy and bureaucratic administration. The monarchy had already neutralized the nobility by gaining the power to tax without consent of Parliament. The king's power was absolute and was exercised through a vast number of public officials recruited by him and in his name. Feudalism had disappeared long before and new forms of land tenure had appeared. The financial charges which weighed most heavily on the people were not the few holdovers from feudal days but the exactions and labour demanded in lieu of taxes by the king's service, particularly under Louis XIV.

The political, social, and economic system of New France had been conceived by high officials of the king in somewhat the same way as a modern government would plan a colony on a distant planet. Colonial policy sought a permanent base for the pursuit of the fur trade and the exploration of the interior of the North American continent. This required a population large enough to provide manpower for supply, trade, transportation, and defence. The coordination of commercial and military expansion was the responsibility of the governor, while administration and public order were those of the intendant. It was the latter who applied the steady stream of directives from Paris on such matters as the location of buildings, the areas assigned to individual farmers, and even appointments in the colonial service. By itself, the colony was of little importance. It was merely a base of operations for an ambitious project: the establishment of a vast commercial empire ranging across the continent and resting on the northern fur trade and on southern plantation agriculture. New France's society and government were tailored to these aims.

The method chosen to encourage settlement along the St. Lawrence River was inspired by the feudal system but was nevertheless very different from it. The French seigneur had been a figure of civil and military authority during the Middle Ages; by the seventeenth century he had lost all his power but retained a superior social position. The Canadian seigneur was basically a land agent drawing modest revenues from land granted in feudal tenure by the king. He was given a monopoly of certain communal services such as milling and baking. He had certain obligations such as road construction and maintenance. Land was held jointly by the seigneur and the *censitaire*, or farmer, who paid tithes and other feudal dues. The seigneur had to give his permission before a *censitaire* could subdivide or sell his land. Unlike his French counterparts, the Canadian seigneur was subject to periodic inspections by the king's officials. If he was thought to be remiss in the recruitment of settlers, or if he proved incapable of meeting the requirements of the original land grant, he was liable to be dispossessed.

New France was a pre-capitalist society under the administrative control of Paris. Its social and economic organization was bound to have a profound influence on mentalities and life styles. One of the main characteristics of this system inspired from feudalism was that it offered few investment outlets for personal savings. Depending on circumstances it was possible for a *censitaire* to acquire land for the establishment of his sons. But he could not easily accumulate wealth by investing his savings in property. He tended to spend his income on consumer goods and services, practically the only area where it was possible to distinguish oneself. The administrative and social control instituted under French rule tended to promote conformism and egalitarianism. And though bureaucratic supervision disappeared under British rule, French society in Canada remained very much the same.

Even before the Conquest in 1759, there were important differences of mentality between French and English settlers in North America which many travellers had noted. One of these, F. X. Charlevoix, a Jesuit priest, compared the two groups in an account of his travels which appeared in Paris in 1744: "There is in New England and in the other provinces of the British Empire a great wealth from which people do not seem to know how to profit; and in New France, a hidden poverty under a natural air of affluence. Commerce and the cultivation of plantations strengthens the former; the industrious nature of the inhabitants is what sustains the latter. The English settler accumulates wealth and makes no superfluous expenditures; the French settler enjoys what he has and often makes a show of what he does not own. The former works for his heirs while the latter leaves them to fend for themselves, very much as he himself has had to do."[1]

The most controversial aspect of the seigneurial system was its hindrance of economic progress and of improvements in agricultural productivity by preventing land from being turned into capital. The main obstacle was its joint ownership by the seigneur and the *censitaire*. The *Coutume de Paris*, the French common law, did not require that mortgages be reported to land registry offices. It was therefore impossible to know the extent to which a property might be mortgaged. The lender, if one could be found in these unfavourable circumstances, was completely dependent on the word of the borrower as to his solvency. Property rights were also diminished by various legal provisions such as the right of relatives and heirs of a deceased person to recover within a fixed period of time, and at cost, any land or property previously sold by him. These restrictions greatly reduced the incentive to accumulate capital.

The practical difficulties of converting land into capital constituted the main grievance levelled against the seigneurial system and the French common law by the English merchant class. They vigorously pressed for the abolition of what they referred to as the feudal system. In their repeated attempts to influence the British governors at home and the Imperial Parliament in London, the merchants blamed the archaic social system and the backward mentality of the French in Lower Canada for the poor economic performance of the colony. They also complained that the seigneurs often failed to provide services in line with the rents and tithes they collected; roads in particular were sometimes so poor as to paralyse commerce completely.

The absence of a system of law adequate for commercial relations resulted in almost unmanageable difficulties for the English merchants. They had to follow the principles and precedents of French common law, which failed to recognize the growing complexity of economic activities. The stubborn refusal of the French political elites in the Assembly to support reform of the colony's system of law and land tenure was a source of profound animosity and encouraged the idea that French and English were two incompatible societies.

The decision by French colonial authorities not to provide a coherent system of commercial law is a clear indication that New France was not meant to attract an independent and populous settlement as was New England. It was designed as a tightly controlled base of military and commercial operations in the New

World. After the Conquest in 1759, the colonial population used the rigid framework which had been imposed on New France to defend itself against foreign capitalism and modernization. It sought to ensure its cultural survival by means of an almost impenetrable shell of archaic laws.

The crisis that finally erupted in armed rebellion in 1837 had long been sensed by French society in Lower Canada. By 1830, more than half of the more prosperous seigneuries were in the hands of English owners who had acquired the seigneurial rights. The French *censitaires*, backed by their political leaders, feared that reform or abolition of the seigneurial system would be at their expense and in favour of English speculators. Their fears were based on the growing tendency of the seigneurs, of the British governors, and even of the magistrature, to consider the *censitaires* simply as tenants and to deny them the co-ownership inherent in the feudal and seigneurial systems. This was an important factor in the growing rigidity of French society and in its resistance to any change in the spirit and the letter of the law. The system had long provided effective protection to a society relatively poor in capital and entrepreneurship.

The external pressures of English capitalism were heightened by a growing internal crisis resulting from excessive subdivision of land and from the absence of local outlets for surplus manpower. Over-population in the seigneuries obviously called for reform of the institutions and laws of Lower Canada, so obviously that speculation intensified and helped increase the charges that weighed upon the *censitaires*. It was suddenly clear to all that French society was disintegrating fairly rapidly.

The collective anxiety which gripped French society in the first quarter of the nineteenth century stemmed from the fact that the preservation of the seigneurial system seemed as dangerous as a reform that to all appearances would dispossess the class that worked the land and enhance the economic power of the English merchant class. Therefore, when the Rebellion broke out in 1837, there was little agreement on the cause that was being promoted. Some of those who took up arms thought they were defending the seigneurial system while others next to them on the firing line wanted to do away with tithes, rents, and the French common law. Others believed they were reviving the spirit of the American Revolution of sixty years before. However, they were united on one point: their implacable opposition to the capitalism of the English merchants and of the British governors.

The nationalist struggle of the period was waged mainly by a class of professionals who had gained the confidence of the population through their higher education and the importance of the services they rendered. Lawyers, notaries, and doctors completely eclipsed the seigneurs and the clergy in popular esteem, and they naturally assumed the ideological leadership of Lower Canada. They were able to take advantage of the ineptness of the Constitutional Act of 1791 which had granted a representative assembly while refusing responsible government. The result was political chaos. While the Assembly was dominated by French nationalists, the executive branch of government was in the hands of the governor and his advisers, hand-picked from the English merchant class. The civil service was entirely English. Those who were most vigorously opposed to the laws voted by the Assembly were the very people called upon to put them into effect.

So relentless was the opposition between the government and the Assembly that the latter had no scruples in openly arranging the tax system to favour the French majority. It exempted land from taxation, so that farmers and professionals made no direct contributions to the colonial treasury. The only taxes which the Assembly was ready to approve were those falling on imports, exports, and transportation. They all applied to English-dominated commerce. In this way the people who had to bear the greater part of the tax burden were the merchants engaged in the fur trade, the Western Indians who supplied the pelts, and the whole population of Upper Canada, whose imports and exports had to go through the port of Montreal. The Assembly, out of hostility to the English commercial system and fear of its impact on French culture, also refused to vote the funds necessary for improving navigation on the St. Lawrence River, on which Upper Canada was already spending considerable sums.

Such was the animosity between French and English that even the administration of justice was paralysed. It frequently happened that jurors in certain types of cases would refuse to find a compatriot guilty. In the Assembly itself, members of the party of the Patriotes sometimes submitted their bitterest political opponents to public inquiries whose doubtful verdicts were often designed to exclude them from public office.

On the eve of the Rebellion in 1837, the French population of Lower Canada numbered 450,000 and the growing English population 150,000. Upper Canada, now Ontario, had an entirely English population of 400,000. The Montreal merchants saw in these figures the answer to their problems: they began agitating for a political union of the two Canadas so that the French, made a minority in a new assembly, would be unable to impede commerce and obstruct government policy. The Imperial Parliament was loath to accede for fear of pushing the French into the American Union. But the 1837 Rebellion played into the hands of the merchants. Its repression brought about the collapse of French political power in the colony. The Act of Union of 1840 enabled an English majority in Upper and Lower Canada to take control of political institutions in the expectation that the stubborn and backward French would eventually be assimilated and their anti-economic system of laws done away with.

In the report that he drafted at the request of the imperial authorities on the causes of the tensions in Canada and their possible resolution, Lord Durham accepted the unfavourable views held about the French by the English population and the merchants. The opinions he expressed more than a hundred years ago still find a sort of folkloric echo today in letters to the editors of Canadian newspapers and on various open-line radio shows. The tensions between the two language communities seem to have retained much of their original causes and of their early manifestations.

Writing about the French in Lower Canada, Durham complained about their opposition to progress: "They clung to ancient prejudices, ancient customs and ancient laws, not from any strong sense of their beneficial effects, but with the unreasoning tenacity of an uneducated and unprogressive people.... They remain an old and stationary society, in a new and and progressive world."[2] He did not see how such a society could survive much longer.

"There can hardly be conceived a nationality more destitute of all that can invigorate and elevate a people than that which is exhibited by the descendants of the French in Lower Canada, owing to their retaining their peculiar language and manners. They are a people with no history, and no literature,"[3] he wrote, alluding to the fact that it was immigrants from France who were responsible for newspapers and other publications in Lower Canada. "It is to elevate them from that inferiority that I desire to give to the Canadians our English character,"[4] he also wrote, referring to the effects which a legislative union of Upper and Lower Canada might be expected to have.

Durham also fully agreed with the views which the English in Canada entertained about themselves and which they still express in the defence of their present status in Quebec:

> The ancient trade of the country was conducted on a much larger and more profitable scale; and new branches of industry were explored. The active and regular habits of the English capitalist drove out of all the more profitable kinds of industry their inert and careless competitors of the French race; but in respect of the greater part (almost the whole) of the commerce and manufactures of the country, the English cannot be said to have encroached on the French; for, in fact, they created employments and profits which had not previously existed. A few of the ancient race smarted under the loss occasioned by the success of English competition; but all felt yet more acutely the gradual increase of a class of strangers in whose hands the wealth of the country appeared to centre, and whose expenditure and influence eclipsed those of the class which had previously occupied the first position in the country.[5]

The French defence of the seigneurial system with its anti-economic bias that hindered progress was inspired mainly by the oppressive nature of contemporary capitalism. The commercialization of a few resources such as wheat and lumber placed the French population at the mercy of speculators, intermediaries, and the vagaries of the international situation. There was opposition to the direction of public expenditures which systematically favoured large and costly works to the detriment of local improvements. But the most galling aspect of the situation was the obvious collusion between the executive branch of the government and the English merchant class, to exclude the French from both government and business.

At the time of the Rebellion, however, the seigneurial system could no longer serve as a rampart against English economic penetration. Overpopulation and emigration to the United States had rendered the French population extremely vulnerable to impoverishment and demoralization. Industrialization, which was beginning at that time, provided some relief to this beleaguered society. But an antiquated system of laws and the speculation encouraged by the coming demise of the seigneurial system stood in the way of industrial development.

In 1854, after the union of the provinces of Canada, the system of land tenure and of laws imposed by France in the seventeenth century was finally abolished. The French retained enough political power to ensure that ownership of the land would pass to the farmers and not to the former seigneurs, who by then were mostly English. The disappearance of the age-old system removed the constraints under which French society had lived for so long. While enjoying some of the benefits of industrialization, the French regrouped into an agricultural society based on the rural parish, existing in parallel with the commercial society of the English. The political alliance between the French leader Louis-Hippolyte Lafontaine and the Upper-Canadian reformer Robert Baldwin enabled French Canada to participate in government patronage and, with this support, to begin developing its own entrepreneurial class.

Little by little the tensions which had given rise to the Rebellion subsided. But the condemnation of English economic behaviour remained as strong as ever, and to this day continues to fuel French nationalism.

Economic Conflict
and Capitalism

Political behaviour in Canada has always been closely linked to attitudes to economic development. On the French side, there is an intellectual distrust of capitalism and a certain disdain for business activities. The problem is the difficulty of integrating economic pursuits identified as being English into a French cultural and social framework. Periods of conflict or stagnation encourage French elites to obstruct political processes in order to promote collective isolation.

Leadership on the English side has always been concerned with channelling collective energies towards economic development, but in a direction very different from that taken in the United States. At all periods of Canadian history, growth has relied heavily on speculation and promotion, and has seldom displayed the kind of entrepreneurship that could have ensured a more balanced development and better served the needs of local populations across the country. Official policy has always aimed at preserving a semi-colonial dependence on Great Britain and later on the United States. Even within Canada itself, the West was long administered as a sub-colony of the East, which illustrates how economic relations have been seen in this country.

The economics of British North America helped shape political behaviour. Heavy reliance on outside markets for a few staples such as furs, wheat, and lumber encouraged the growth of speculative and promotional activities in marketing and transportation. These in turn favoured the rise of business factions, the practice of secrecy, the quest for privileged access to power, and a very close identification with the executive branch of government. As information and influence became far more important than competence, public administration grew jealous of its secrets and would share them only with friends. Indeed, Canadian history in the eighteenth and nineteenth centuries is the history of the collusion between political authorities and the agents of economic growth. Official policies, together with the attitudes of financial leaders, consistently displayed a great deal of intolerance towards any cultural attitudes which might stand in the way of investments and growth.

As a result of their historical interaction, English and French have agreed on one point: economics and culture are two fundamentally opposed realms. Because of their traditional animosity, there has been an irresistible tendency among them to choose one to the exclusion of the other. This is the battleground that Lord Durham referred to when he wrote about "two nations warring within the bosom of a single state," a statement which René Lévesque echoed more than a hundred years later speaking of "two scorpions in a bottle."

The course of Canadian history has been determined by pressure and resistance and by a struggle that has never been resolved to the satisfaction of one side or the other. After England had taken over the French territories of North America it was thought that the Royal Proclamation of 1763 would settle the fate of New France. The fur trade was opened up to the merchants of Albany and New York and the very profitable fisheries of the Gulf of St. Lawrence were assigned to Newfoundland and Nova Scotia. The former French colony was reduced to a narrow strip of territory on each side of the St. Lawrence River, from what is now the Ontario border to a point beyond

Anticosti Island. It was confidently expected that the arrival of English settlers would soon swamp the French population. Assimilation was thought to be inevitable because of the progressive character of English commercial law and the enterprising spirit of English merchants.

However, the integration of New France into the British Empire could not be achieved in this manner. The harshness of the climate did not favour rapid and intensive settlement, British immigrants preferring the warmer colonies to the south. The English merchants who had come to Montreal and Quebec City began commercializing agricultural production and taking advantage of Montreal's favourable geographical location to break into the fur trade. To their dismay, they soon realized that Canada's narrow boundaries, and the crippling limitations resulting from imperial policies, meant that the colony was not viable. The French population resented official attempts at assimilation, and it watched with a certain interest the growing rebelliousness of New England and other American colonies. Concerned about the loyalty of Canada and eager to preserve their access to the West, colonial authorities did a complete about-turn with the promulgation of the Quebec Act in 1774.

Almost resigned to the loss of its older North American colonies, England began to act as if she were simply the heir of France in the New World. The first step in implementing the policies of the former colonial power was to recognize the geography that had made New France a base of operations for penetration of the continental heartland. The immense commercial possibilities of the fur trade determined British policy as they had France's. The borders of Canada were restored to what they had been before the fall of Quebec in 1759. As the French had been before them, the British became the allies of the Western Indians against the encroachments of settlers from the surplus population of New England

and Virginia. Thanks to their preferential access to British markets and capital, English merchants in Montreal quickly assumed the economic leadership of Canada.

In order to achieve her new imperial designs, England needed the active support of the French population, for the settlement and defence of Canada and for keeping the country beyond the reach of the impending American Revolution. Only the French of Canada were able to restore the former alliance with the Western Indians, who retained an unbounded confidence in France. In addition, their expertise was needed in the fur trade.

The Quebec Act of 1774 restored French rights abrogated by the Royal Proclamation of 1763. French laws and customs were restored, including the semi-feudal system of land tenure. The British, who had been on the point of instituting popular and democratic government by means of an elected assembly, held back in favour of a governor whose powers were similar to those of his French predecessors. The imperial government, in its imitation of French colonial policies, even refrained from creating municipal councils for fear they might eventually challenge the powers of the governor, as had already happened in the thirteen rebellious colonies.

In effect, the Quebec Act forced English and French to share the same territory and to come to some accommodation with each other. Under the circumstances each group assumed a particular function or role: one was in charge of commerce and of the economy while the other was to be in charge of laws and of social organization in so far as they did not interfere with economic development. This was the first time that there appeared in Canadian history the notion of collective vocations, a concept that remained almost unchallenged until well into the twentieth century. For a very long time the notion of ethnic domains remained the foundation of English-French cooperation, surviving several constitutional upheavals.

During the early years of British rule, the governors were generally sympathetic to the French. Because of their aristocratic background, they usually preferred the cultured French elites to the rough and acquisitive English merchants. But impatience and aloofness gradually set in. The conservatism of French elites and their inability to grasp economic ideas seemed to threaten the progress of the country. Their unusual quickness to take offence gradually undermined the kind of compact suggested by the Quebec Act. The governors gradually moved to the side of the English merchant class, thereby forging that long-lasting alliance between the executive power of government and those who managed the economy.

This new alliance was to last throughout most of Canada's subsequent history. It was to prove a stumbling block to a permanent and workable understanding with the French. The very evidence of this alliance between political authority and capital shocked the values of French society. It tended to see the governor as the representative of royal authority which was expected to remain above political disputes and economic rivalries. The king's representative was supposed to arbitrate conflicting claims of economic and social needs. From that point on, French elites could never be shaken in their belief that the managers of the economy had perverted the country's political system.

Increasing difficulties in coming to terms with the French led to the Constitutional Act of 1791. While the Act continued to recognize French laws and customs, it severely restricted the scope of their application by splitting the country into Upper and Lower Canada. The Act also made a few concessions to democratic sentiments seeping in from the United States by establishing a popularly elected Assembly. However, it failed to grant responsible government, that is, an executive power relying on the support of a majority in the Assembly.

The justification of this omission was very simple. The imperial government did not want to do anything that might eventually interfere with the working alliance between executive authority and economic power in the colony. The geography of British North America and British commercial interests conspired to maintain the mercantilist and authoritarian policies which France had initiated more that 150 years before.

The particular form of government put into effect by the Constitutional Act, opposing the executive authority of the governor to the political influence of the Assembly, confirmed the fundamental opposition between English capitalism and French society. It intensified forms of political behaviour which were to survive the traumatic experience of the 1837 Rebellion. Because laws and moneys were voted by the Assembly, to be implemented and spent by the governor and his council, the French majority discovered that, although it could not impose its views, it could easily paralyse the administration of the country. The English minority of Lower Canada swore that some day it would get the better of this obstinate and obstructive people.

The abuses associated with the economic system, particularly those stemming from the collusion of the governor and the English merchant class, were noted by Lord Durham in his report on the causes of the 1837 Rebellion.

> The circumstances of the early colonial administration excluded the native Canadian from power, and vested all offices of trust and emolument in the hands of strangers of English origin. The highest posts in the law were confided to the same class of persons. The functionaries of the civil government, together with the officers of the army, composed a kind of privileged class,

occupying the first place in the community, and excluding the higher class of the natives from society, as well as from the government of their own country. It was not till within a very few years, as was testified by persons who had seen much of the country, that this society of civil and military functionaries ceased to exhibit towards the higher order of Canadians an exclusiveness of demeanour, which was more revolting to a polite and sensitive people than the monopoly of power and profit; nor was this national favouritism discontinued, until after repeated complaints and an angry contest, which had excited passions that concessions could not allay.[1]

Thus wrote the man who in the end had so little esteem for the French that he believed the most charitable way of saving them from their own backwardness was to assimilate them into an English majority.

When looking at Lower Canada, Durham saw the sorry state of that province as originating in the fact of "two nations warring within the bosom of a single state." The two ethnic camps each had their stronghold from which they could not be routed. But when he looked at the causes of the Rebellion in Upper Canada, Durham discovered that similar abuses prevailed in the absence of ethnic rivalries and of antiquated laws such as the French had in Lower Canada. The collusion between economic and political interests, together with the absence of democratic local institutions to check abuses of power, were clearly at fault. Durham dealt at length with the concentration of power in the hands of the Family Compact, as the financial and social elite of Upper Canada was known at that time.

For a long time this body of men, receiving at times accessions to its numbers, possessed almost all the highest public offices, by means of which, and of its influence in the Executive Council, it

wielded all the powers of government; it maintained influence in the legislature by means of its
predominance in the Legislative Council; and it
disposed of the large number of petty posts which
are in the patronage of the government all over
the Province. Successive governors, as they came
in their turn, are said to have either submitted
quietly to its influence, or, after a short and
unavailing struggle, to have yielded to this
well-organized party the real conduct of affairs.
The bench, the magistracy, the high offices of the
Episcopal Church, and a great part of the legal
profession, are filled by the adherents of this
party: by grant or purchase, they have acquired
nearly the whole of the waste lands of the
province; they are all powerful in the chartered
banks, and, till lately, shared among themselves
almost exclusively all offices of trust and profit.[2]

The ruinous consequences of such a situation
were obvious to Durham. He noted in his report how
public expenditures generally favoured private
interests at the expense of the common good. This was
true of Upper Canada and of Newfoundland, Nova
Scotia, and New Brunswick. For example, the funds
required to support a network of elementary schools
in Upper Canada were expended mainly on the
University of Toronto, whose social and geographical
accessibility was strictly limited. Investments in
communications benefited mostly the merchants and
speculators who shipped agricultural products and
lumber to British markets, rather than the local
producers. Very little was spent to assist farmers or
improve local conditions. Crown lands were distrib-
uted to political friends who kept them idle and
uncultivated for speculation. These practices stood in
the way of intensive settlement. In most parts of
Upper Canada as well as in other British colonies,
villages seldom acquired a large enough population to
ensure the economic maintenance of mills, schools,
roads, churches, and a host of other services on which
rural life depends.

During the 1830s, public debt in Upper Canada was so high that government revenues could not meet interest payments. The larger part of the debt was incurred in the construction of canals along the St. Lawrence River and the Great Lakes. The government of Upper Canada, influenced by promoters and contractors, gave its financial backing to many projects without ensuring that Lower Canada was willing to go ahead with the complementary work on its section of the river. But the Assembly of Lower Canada, dominated as it was by French representatives uncompromisingly hostile to English capitalism, refused to cooperate and to vote the required funds. Upper Canada was therefore saddled with totally unproductive assets whose costs had ballooned out of all proportion because of poor planning, incompetence, and official corruption. These works constituted an exorbitant charge on the provincial economy.

As a consequence of this mismanagement, industry and commerce stagnated. The value of land in the British colonies was only a fraction of that in adjacent areas of the United States. Not only was it becoming increasingly difficult to attract British investment, but people and capital were leaving the colonies. The more dynamic elements of society sought a political and economic system that adequately rewarded work and was free of the constraints of speculation and favouritism. Canada and the other British colonies had remained untouched by the democratic sentiments and the entrepreneurial spirit which had brought about the American Revolution some sixty years earlier.

The old colonies had managed to overthrow a system which subordinated their interests to those of England and the Empire. Before 1776, the colonies had little influence on the prices offered for their products on imperial markets or on those they had to pay for vital imports. In addition, legal and fiscal obstacles inhibited intercolonial trade and helped maintain the privileged position of metropolitan producers. The British governors were the defenders of this mercantilist system. The patronage they controlled was meant to promote acceptance of the system and participation in it.

In New England, as opposed to the South where plantation agriculture prevailed, the Revolution had an agrarian character. It defended agricultural interests against speculative and monopolistic trade practices. It sought to promote a harmonious type of local development that went against the regional economic specialization which imperial policies tried to impose. The Revolution sought to extend popular control over all levels of public administration, and it introduced a beneficial distinction between the government's responsibilities towards the population in general and towards the agents of economic development. As a result, the United States acquired a better equilibrium between local and national interests, a certain degree of democracy in its economic system, and a dramatic improvement in public morality.

However, the abuses which the American Revolution sought to eliminate survived in Canada. Colonial rule became more oppressive. The massive influx of political refugees from the United States, the United Empire Loyalists, as they were known, contributed immeasurably to a heightening of tensions in Lower Canada towards the end of the eighteenth century. The Loyalists exhibited a strong anti-French bias resulting from more than a century of frontier wars against New France. They were closely identified with the social and economic system which the American Revolution had overthrown and which French political leaders in Lower Canada resented bitterly. The existence of the two language communities on the same territory proved to be increasingly difficult, so that when the Rebellion broke out in 1837 the English were mercilessly pictured as oppressive and the French as backward.

After the Rebellion had been crushed, the union of Upper and Lower Canada was seen as the only way to preserve imperial authority and ensure a lasting peace in the colony. This objective would be reached by putting the French in a minority in the new Assembly of the United Provinces of Canada, thereby encouraging its assimilation by an English-speaking majority. The imperial government was determined to break the obstruction of the Assembly of Lower Canada, to ease the financial problems of Upper Canada, and to do away once and for all with the French common law and its anti-economic bias.

Once again, however, the French were saved by developments in England and in North America. It was during this period that power in England passed from the hands of a commercial oligarchy and landed gentry to a new class of industrial capitalists. The latter pressed irresistibly to end the old protectionist and mercantilist system, and sought to promote England's industrial leadership by means of an aggressive policy of free trade. At the same time, continental Europe was going through a series of uncontrollable political convulsions as various groups of democrats, nationalists, and communists attempted to deal with the effects of the industrial revolution. In North America, the growing economic power of the United States encouraged a policy of territorial expansion which could prove extremely dangerous for Canada, particularly if internal tensions were allowed to subsist.

The Union government, which had been created in 1840 to ensure the maintenance of colonial and imperial policies and to submerge the French, was forced to change course. It had to go ahead with a series of reforms which dramatically altered the conduct of public affairs, the nature of economic activity, and the shared exercise of power in the colony. In 1845, the governor accepted the creation of municipal and school councils, thereby depriving himself and his allies of an important part of their political patronage. In 1846, the Assembly of the United Provinces petitioned the Imperial Parliament to restore French language rights, a request which was granted in 1849. By that time it was obvious to everyone that only conciliation could ensure peace and prosperity.

A year earlier, the governor of the United Provinces had broken new constitutional ground. Lord Elgin sent a joint invitation to the Reform leader of Upper Canada, Robert Baldwin, and to the nationalist leader of Lower Canada, Louis-Hippolyte Lafontaine, asking them jointly to form a new cabinet. This was the first time in Canada that the principle of responsible or representative government had been recognized. Significantly, it also ushered in a new era in the relations between English and French.

Canada being at that time a unitary state, the double invitation from Lord Elgin constituted an implicit recognition of the binational character of the country, that is, of the necessity for the government to rally a majority of voters in both Upper and Lower Canada, and among both the English and the French. It was obvious to most people then that the country could not prosper without a fairly high degree of cooperation between the two language groups. Fortunately, political equality was fairly easy to work out because at that time the two parts of the country were almost equal in numbers, as were the English and the French.

The main architect of this new alliance was Baldwin. After the defeat of the Rebellion in Upper and Lower Canada, and after the initial hardening of imperial policy, he came to the conclusion that a coalition of progressive elements in both parts of the country could take power. His ultimate purpose was to reform Canadian political institutions and reorient public policies so as to subject the most far-reaching social and economic decisions of the government to popular approval and to make public spending serve the general good rather than private interests.

As for Lafontaine, the alliance seemed natural. The ill-considered recourse to arms in 1837 and 1838 and its brutal repression had completely demoralized the French population and opened the way for vengeful reprisals. Lafontaine believed that with the help of Baldwin it might be possible to reverse official policies. Naturally enough, his first objective was to re-establish the French language in the Assembly. Lafontaine also wanted greater French participation in the administration of Lower Canada. But this proved to be a thornier problem. The compromise which finally prevailed, and which Lafontaine accepted, was the creation of dual ministries for the differing social and cultural needs of Upper and Lower Canada. However, departments of national importance, such as the treasury and the militia, remained English. Lafontaine understood that this was the best deal possible under the circumstances.

However, the most crucial issue was of a different order altogether. Overpopulation in the seigneuries combined with the agricultural depression of the 1830s to bring about an unprecedented level of French emigration to New England, whose industry provided jobs for those who could no longer make a living from the land. At the same time, boatloads of Irish families were arriving in Canada, driven from their country by famine. This dual problem could be resolved only by promoting new industrial activities to absorb the surplus manpower. It meant that French people would have to begin looking at their society in economic terms, and allow English investors and managers to develop the natural resources of the province and make use of its labour.

In the eyes of the French population, this new type of capitalism seemed less threatening than the old commercial one. Instead of resting on the speculative ownership of land, or on manipulative activities such as buying and selling, the new economic order appeared to have more acceptable foundations in the form of know-how, capital, and labour. It seemed to produce more than private wealth, to bring well-being to all. These were notions easily grasped by the French population, which saw nothing very radical or threatening in Lafontaine's program. The majority supported it and even pressed for changes that would give a new lease on life to a defeated and demoralized society. Industrialization became a way of ending the long and wilful isolation which had preceded the Rebellion and which had eventually endangered the very survival of French society.

By promoting a new spirit of cooperation with the English, Lafontaine expected that the French would eventually become participants in the new economic order ushered in by the industrial revolution. More than that, he hoped that the political partnership with Baldwin and the progressive elements of Upper Canada would ultimately produce an economic partnership with Canadian capitalists. By obtaining their fair share of government patronage, the French, he thought, would be able to accumulate the kind of capital necessary to support a new class of entrepreneurs able to keep abreast of their English counterparts.

One reason why such a vision could never be entirely realized was that, even though Canada experienced the industrial revolution, until quite recently it never really became an industrial country. Well into the twentieth century, its prosperity was founded upon the export of agricultural products and natural resources. As a result, patterns of transportation, investment, and economic development continued to follow the broad lines established in the days of the fur trade and of the commercial empire of the St. Lawrence. The imperatives of the export trade continued to dominate politics, public spending, and the whole tone of Canadian life.

Given the historical factors behind Canadian prosperity, the most important activity in the development of the national economy was promotional. Politicians and bankers worked hand in hand to sell investment opportunities in Britain and in the United States. The capital, the expertise, and the skills necessary for the growth of the country came mostly from abroad. The great prime ministers, such as John A. Macdonald, were those who could project a vision of the country's future. Vision meant public works and jobs for the voters, and it brought enormous profits to investors and promoters. It was the key to power.

In this manner the construction of canals and railways perpetuated the conditions associated with the old commercial and mercantilist order of the eighteenth century that Lord Durham had noted and condemned. The highly speculative nature of Canadian economic development encouraged the growth of financial in-groups controlling information and sharing it only with friends and allies. At the same time, the tendency towards the concentration of economic power became very strong. Inevitably, the new industrial capitalism reproduced the main characteristics of the old order that the French had fought so bitterly. In this context it proved unrealistic to expect a permanent change in English-French relations.

Not surprisingly, by the end of the 1860s the Union government was threatened with complete paralysis, just as its predecessor in Upper Canada had been in the 1830s, and this for reasons that were quite similar. Once again, public spending became concentrated on highly speculative national investments such as canals and railways, to the detriment of local improvements necessary for the well-being of the population. The classic symptom of poor management of public affairs finally appeared: the national debt was pushed to the point where interest on it began to outstrip the capacity of taxpayers. The French, therefore, resumed their obstruction of political processes. The high taxation imposed upon them went only to support investments from whose profits they were systematically excluded.

Confederation solved the debt problem of the Union government by bringing the Maritime provinces into a broader union, thereby increasing the number of taxpayers on which Canada's capacity for debt repayment ultimately rested. The corresponding increase in the number of voters helped swamp the French in the new Parliament and effectively prevented the possibility that they might once more obstruct the workings of the political system. But they were bribed and pacified with the grant of a certain measure of autonomy within the Quebec preserve. The province was given control over its civil laws, its social and cultural institutions, and its natural resources. It had enough freedom to create the kind of society it wanted on its own territory.

As a political compromise, Confederation turned out to be very astute and durable. It ensured political peace for a hundred more years, and it gave a free hand to financial interests eager to open up the West. French society withdrew into a new cocoon, a protective shell within which security was provided by the social life of the rural parish and by the leadership of the Catholic clergy. Ethnic solidarity, the preservation of French language and culture, religion, the ownership of agricultural land, all these were elements of an ideology that was overwhelmingly preoccupied with collective survival. And, in this regard, there were a number of threats to be warded off.

Industrialization turned out to be a mixed blessing. It provided jobs for surplus population, but it undermined the cohesion and solidarity of French society. Factory work was a new discipline that had to be learned. The chain of command in many industries demanded a loyalty that competed, as it were, with that required by traditional institutions such as the Church, the family, and the parish, and by the whole

tenor of rural life. Industrialization introduced insta-
bility and tensions by displacing the old feelings about
one's place and role in society, and substituting newer
notions of careers and upward mobility. The intricate
relationships of a traditional society were eroded by
the new practice of terminating the moral and
psychological indebtedness associated with services
rendered by means of a payment in money, particularly with respect to professional services rendered by
doctors, lawyers, and others. For the vast majority,
industrialization was a disorienting experience, and it
led the French elites into somewhat contradictory
attitudes.

Nationalist elements and the clergy were allied in
condemning industrial society, the dangers of the
large city, the depredations of big business, and the
immoral nature of modernity in all its guises. They
dug in their heels, and they were of one mind in
preserving the predominance of the rural vote in
provincial politics by a margin of almost two to one
over the urban vote. This unbalanced representation
ended only in 1960.

By then Quebec had experienced an upsetting
exodus from the countryside to the city. Indeed, the
long-standing rurally oriented ideology that had provided shelter for more than a hundred years could no
longer do so. The French had to come out of their
cocoon and make their peace with the industrial
society that had overwhelmed them, but in the
process it was inevitable that they would have to
challenge the English for economic domination of that
society.

Individual and Collective Rights

In his book *Quebec in Question*, Quebec sociologist Marcel Rioux observes that the English have been individualists and the French have been collectivists, and that this important difference has always set them apart.[1] In the eighteenth and nineteenth centuries, this was particularly true and the distinction was based on the attitudes of each group to property. For the English, land was a marketable commodity that individuals could mortgage or sell, while for the French, who clung to the seigneurial system until 1854, land belonged to the community.

With the rise of the industrial and consumer societies in the nineteenth and twentieth centuries, this distinction between individualists and collectivists lost much of its meaning. Today's English businessman is as attached to his large corporation as a French civil servant is to the Quebec government. Neither is individualistic and both accept the hierarchies and ideologies of these two types of bureaucracies, one private and the other public.

Nevertheless, the idea of the English as individualists and the French as collectivists resurfaced in the public mind toward the end of the 1960s. This coincided with the language conflict which threatened to rearrange the powers of English and French in Quebec and Canada. The English led the defence of the status quo, and in the name of individual rights fought for freedom to choose language of schooling.

French nationalists, on the other hand, invoked the idea of collective rights to affirm the primacy of the French language in Quebec and to curb freedom to choose language of schooling. Through this political debate individual and collective rights returned as guiding ideas for the two groups.

For the English, only individuals have rights in Canada; the society is the sum of individuals with equal rights. The English are loath to recognize special rights for groups, and do not see why minority cultures should be encouraged in a cultural framework that happens to be predominantly English. Although Quebec is majority French, the English community feels that the province must be considered part of the Canadian framework, that as a result they have the same individual rights as Ontarians or Albertans, and that these include the right to work and to go to school in English. To defend the use of English in schools and corporate management, the community also employs arguments based on the British traditions of economic liberalism and civil liberties. Through this reasoning it criticizes the French for not being properly initiated into democracy as practised in North America.

These ideas are regularly reflected in the speeches of senior Montreal business executives. The chairman of the Royal Bank of Canada, W. Earle McLaughlin, declared in a talk before the French Chambre de Commerce on the language question that surely French Canadians had entered "into the North American lifestyle in the sense that they take for granted some of the fundamental freedoms so characteristic of the North American scene." Entering into the heart of his subject, Bill 101, he said that "these include freedom of movement and freedom of speech with relatively little in the way of massive government regulations or intervention in their daily lives." Then he asked whether Quebec wanted "an open society with freedom to choose one's language and lifestyle" or a "closed, planned, and regulated society in which certain basic freedoms are abridged."

Top English education officials in Quebec take a similar approach. The views of spokesmen for the Protestant School Board of Greater Montreal, which strongly opposed the Bill 22 language legislation of Robert Bourassa, illustrate this. Speaking before a commission of the Quebec National Assembly in 1974, the Board's chairman, John Simms, said the proposed law was "just one more Big Daddy attempt by one of our benevolent governments to take over the civil liberties of its people." In its brief to the commission, the Board stated that "it is almost unbelievable that an enlightened government in this day... would not have accepted as fundamental that legislation based on distinction of... language... is a direct denial of the principle that all men are equal before the law," and added that "Bill 22 leads us to pose the question: Is Quebec a democratic society?"

The French also recognize individual rights but only where there is equivalent protection for collective rights. The French contend that as a group they are not participating in important sectors of Quebec life, such as the economy, and that they must impose French in business and the school system to promote their legitimate collective interests.

During the public hearings on Bill 22 most French-speaking groups supported the government's restrictions on access to English-language schooling and called for even further limitations. The parents' association of Ecole St. Ernest in Laval, for example, expressed widespread French thinking when it told the government that "defence of the French national heritage could not be left to the initiative of individual citizens" and that the rights of the French collectivity took precedence over the rights of individuals.

The Ligue des droits et libertés, the most important non-governmental human rights organization in Quebec, took a similar position. The Ligue commented that it was useless to talk of the rights of individuals in certain sectors of Quebec society when social conditions did not allow individuals to develop their personal resources or express their cultural identity. The English believe, however, that the freedom of private enterprise to choose its language of operations takes precedence over whatever group rights the French might have. In their view, economic questions are more important than social ones.

Although collective rights are discussed mainly in connection with the French and the language issue, the concept is by no means new in Canada and already takes many forms. Few contest the right to exist of trade unions or farming cooperatives, for example. These organizations were set up to give certain groups with little power advantages that their members could not attain through individual effort.

It is interesting to note that the principle of collective rights is much more accepted in the United States than in Canada. Class action has for a long time been part of the American legal system, and affirmative-action legislation, which sets employment quotas for disadvantaged groups such as Blacks and women, was passed in the early 1970s. Although affirmative-action rulings have been challenged in the courts on grounds of counter-discrimination, the U.S. in general remains committed to strong programs to eliminate socio-economic disparities between groups.

In Canada, by contrast, class-action law was introduced to Quebec and certain other provinces only recently, and compulsory affirmative action of the American variety does not yet exist. The federal human rights commission can investigate complaints of discrimination and make recommendations to cover groups. Apart from this, however, the principle receives no legislative support, although there are both federal and provincial programs to encourage hiring and promotion of minorities. Generally speaking, the idea of collective rights garners little sympathy in English Canada. The English in Quebec suspect that collective rights further Quebec sovereignty and French invasion of the economic domain, while those outside Quebec feel it could undermine their cultural predominance and power across the country.

The present positions of English and French on individual and collective rights are to a great degree the manifestation of certain contradictory political traditions in the country. English demands for individual rights serve the status quo and the continued dominance of English economic culture. French demands for collective rights would, if accepted, hasten the end of the ethnic stratification which has always existed in Canada and would establish French in all domains of Quebec society.

The English defence of individual rights rests on the historic idea that Canada is English and that rights should be exercised within an English cultural framework.[2] This idea persists in the English community of Quebec, in spite of the presence of the French majority, because the English have always identified their culture with their economic activity, which until recently spanned the country. The notion that the predominance of English is natural and right can be found in Lord Durham, whose report on the 1837 Rebellion suggested that French society was inferior to the English because it could not understand economic problems.

This idea of English superiority has a long history. In the eighteenth century the "rights of Englishmen," as enunciated by Edmund Burke in answer to the French Revolution's "Declaration of the Rights of Man," took precedence over other groups,[3] and Durham's orientation reflects this. The idea received renewed support at the turn of the century from a group of American and British intellectuals and businessmen, known as Social Darwinists, who applied Darwinian theories of biological evolution to social and economic phenomena. These people fostered the idea that the strongest were the most fit to rule, whether in Europe, America, Africa, or Asia. This school of thought encouraged the extension of Anglo-Saxon hegemony throughout the world and exerted considerable influence on Canadian prime ministers from John A. Macdonald on. Their belief in the superiority of English was shown in support for British imperialism, in the treatment of the French minority across the country, and in exclusive identification of economic progress with Anglo-Saxon culture.

The British North America Act showed how the English intended to monopolize power in Canada. As constitutional authority Claude-Armand Sheppard points out, the Act protects majority rather than minority concerns and supports individual to the detriment of collective rights.[4] Article 133 of the Act places English and French on an equal footing at the federal level and in Quebec for language of legislation, parliamentary records, and the courts. But it says nothing about the language of work for the civil service or for communications between the government and the people.

The abrogation of French rights in the West and in Ontario came from a desire for a single English culture. Ontario resolved to colonize the West quickly and wipe out French influence at the time of Confederation and the Métis rebellion led by Louis Riel. The idea that Canada should be English, and English only, was reflected in the ideas of *Toronto Globe* editor George Brown, a strong francophobe and an anti-Catholic. In his push to anglicize the West, Brown in 1869 said: "We hope to see a new Upper Canada in the North West Territory—in its well-regulated society, in its education, morality and religion." The promotion of an exclusively English country was not restricted to conservative minds. Among progressive thinkers who thought this way were J. S. Woodsworth, founder of the Co-operative Commonwealth Federation (CCF) which preceded the New Democratic Party, and John W. Dafoe, editor of the *Winnipeg Free Press*.

This same belief in the superiority of English culture helped lead the Canadian government to lend automatic support for British imperial policies. The French, through Henri Bourassa, fought against this support because they felt Canada should be independent from Britain in economic and foreign policy. For the first sixty years of Confederation, however, the various federal prime ministers, including Sir Wilfrid Laurier, supported British imperialism and, despite the profound disagreement of the French in Quebec, agreed to fight in the Boer War and World War I.

These feelings of cultural superiority have yielded to a certain liberalism in the treatment of the French minority. Old policies have been reversed through the federal Official Languages Act, the partial re-establishment of French school rights in Ontario and Manitoba, the recognition of French as an official language in New Brunswick, and the 1979 Supreme Court decision re-establishing French as an official language of Manitoba's legislature and courts. Nevertheless, strong vestiges of the past remain in the widely held conviction that the economy should remain exclusively English.

Traces of this are evident in the various provincial human rights codes which assume that there is essentially one culture, English, but that all individuals, no matter what their background, have a right to a place in it. What this means is that if a French-speaking person is prepared to set aside his language and his culture, he will have the right to equal treatment in the system. Human rights commissions would pursue companies who refused to hire French-speaking people, for example, but they would not demand that such firms alter language-of-work policies to suit these people.

Because of the assumption that the economy must be English, the federal government has never been able to create French-language units in ministries such as finance or trade and commerce. When the Quebec government sought to impose French as the language of the economy, even on its own territory, it suffered from country-wide criticism.

The federal policy of promoting the multicultural character of Canada is also based on the idea of one prevailing culture. For this reason, it has never been accepted in French Quebec and is perceived by the French across Canada as a betrayal of the English-French compact under which power was supposed to be shared by the two main cultures. The multiculturalism policy suggests that Canada is a mosaic of many ethnicities enjoying equal status and protection under the English cultural umbrella, except for certain concessions to French regionalism in Quebec.

Currently, however, the principal rationalization for the dominance of English culture comes from managers of large national companies in Montreal and elsewhere. These people insist that contemporary industrial society requires the use of English at least in management and scientific research. According to their argument, the Canadian managerial elite, whether in business or the federal civil service, operates in English because the international language of business is English and not because they are attached to English culture. In their view, attempts to impose French as the language of work in Quebec are retrogressive and demonstrate rather folkloric attitudes.

A related line of thinking was expressed by the eminent Canadian sociologist John Porter at a conference sponsored by the Canadian Foundation of Human Rights in Montreal in 1978. Professor Porter, who wrote *The Vertical Mosaic*, suggested that cultural diversity and multiculturalism tend to perpetuate traditional patterns of discrimination according to ethnic origin. According to him, the best strategy for ethnic groups is to forget their heritage and rapidly integrate into the culture of the majority. Professor Porter also opposed promotion of collective rights because he thought it went against modernization and bureaucratic organization.

The idea that even the French in Quebec must accept English as the language of the economy has been shown in statements by all wings of the anglophone elite in Quebec. At the end of the 1960s, John Simms, who at the time was head of the Presbyterian church in Montreal, commented that "the English language is now an absolute necessity from the economic point of view" and that English-speaking people in Quebec "have no alternative but to force more and more people to accept the English system and to learn English."[5] The English elite, whether in business, the universities, or the church, will not admit that its attitudes might come from an attachment to English culture or to a certain chauvinism. Instead, they use the economic argument to justify traditional attitudes and maintenance of the status quo.

The assumption behind this type of statement is that French cannot be the language of business in Quebec because the international language of commerce is English. However, a study published in June 1977 by the Régie de la langue française showed that in Europe head offices of multinational corporations conduct their internal business in the language of the country where they are located. English is used only for communications between companies and divisions.

In contrast to the English, the French always imagined that Confederation was a pact between two equal partners. In reality, however, the constitution simply reflected the power that each group was capable of wielding. At the time of Confederation the English insisted upon economic predominance. Faced with this, the French once more withdrew into their own world for protection from the pressures of industrialization and modernization. The rural and agricultural parish became the centre of French life and remained the focus of Quebec politics until the 1960s.

Ruralism survived too long and Quebec started to suffer from the ill-effects of inadequate modernization.

The Quiet Revolution, which stressed urban values, tried to reverse this. However, attempts to shift the direction of Quebec society led to insecurity for the French population. The rural economy which had been the cornerstone of French culture was withering away when conquest of the urban domain still seemed unattainable. The vulnerability of French society was suddenly apparent and collective survival became an issue. Nationalist thinkers became preoccupied with collective rights, particularly in the predominantly English urban and industrial sector, which was still rather unfamiliar territory.

The affirmation of French collective rights in the economic domain was part of an ambitious program of modernization conducted on many fronts. At the federal level, Pierre Trudeau, Jean Marchand, and Gérard Pelletier, who entered federal politics together in 1965, played important roles in this regard. Their aim was to establish a French presence at the centre of the federal government to promote and reflect the new urban orientation of Quebec. The trio also wanted to widen the field of career possibilities for the French in the public service, an operation which became known in English as "French power." In addition, the French federal politicians set up programs to strengthen the French communities outside Quebec and tried to assure government services for them in their own language.

In Quebec, however, the optimism of the Quiet Revolution waned as it became clear that the conquest of the economy would be long and difficult. Pessimism spread with demographic reports which suggested an eventual decline in the French population due to a falling birth rate and the tendency of immigrants to integrate into the English community. This led to strong demands for legislation to affirm French collective rights and for a re-ordering of the old pact between the two founding peoples.

The first official support for collective rights was

expressed by the Royal Commission on Bilingualism and Biculturalism in the mid-sixties. It recommended that the French outside Quebec acquire the right to education and government services in French as well as the possibility of working in their native language in certain all-French units in the federal civil service in Ottawa. Within Quebec, the Commission advocated implementing a collective right — to speak French at work — in the economic domain, where the language of work was largely English. In the 1970s, the idea gained ground when the Commission of Inquiry on the Position of the French Language and on Language Rights in Quebec started to examine the type of provincial government policies on language which could flow from acceptance of the collective-rights principle. The Gendron Commission, as it was commonly called, was reluctant to recommend legislating against English schooling for newcomers or making French compulsory in business. Nevertheless, the demands of groups who appeared at the commission's public hearings, and its own recognition of the collective-rights idea, inspired Bill 22 in 1974 and Bill 101 in 1977.

The evolution of international law on minorities also favoured the recognition of collective rights. After World War I and the collapse of the Austro-Hungarian Empire, special treaties were signed to try to protect the large minority groups in the newly created states. Although the treaties never worked, the principle of minority rights was recognized. Until the mid-sixties, the United Nations avoided minority-rights issues. The Universal Declaration of Human Rights of 1948 is a document of individual and not collective rights. However, the International Covenant on Economic, Social and Cultural Rights of 1966 is based on collective rights and includes in this the right to self-determination. Ratification of the Covenant coincided with the rise all over the world of minorities in demand of recognition. Those in the West included

Welsh, Scots, Irish, Bretons, Basques, and Jura French, and there were many more in Asia and Africa.

From the Quebec point of view, however, the most important minority-rights development came not from Europe but from the United States. American society has always had a reputation for insisting that newcomers quickly forget their origins and rapidly integrate into the Anglo-Saxon majority. In the past the United States has been characterized as a "melting pot" while Canada was supposed to be a more culturally open "mosaic." However, the facts do not fit this description.

As Canadian sociologist Wallace Clement points out in his book *Continental Corporate Power*, American immigrants were able to climb the social scale faster than Canadian immigrants and were at the same time more successful in retaining distinctive ethnic characteristics. In an interview in the book, a Canadian of non-British origin who became a member of the American corporate elite explained why he left Canada for the United States.

> It appeared to me that the United States had a more fluid society, with greater opportunity for upward mobility—social and economic—than Canada offered at the time. Canadians were then attached to British class rigidities and emphasis upon birth and racial origin—prejudices from which American society was freer, and which I believed would be frustrating handicaps to an ambitious young man. I concluded that my progress in Canada would be slowed by the fact that I was not of British birth, origin or name.[6]

By the early 1960s, there were enough non-Anglo-Saxon people in important positions in the United States to give the traditional Anglo-Protestant culture a new look. The influence of these people grew with the rise of Black nationalism. The Black Power movement with its slogan "Black is beautiful" showed that Blacks would resist assimilation and insist upon conserving their distinctive group identities. Other groups followed and made similar demands. These minorities pushed American society to become more pluralist and more accepting of cultural diversity in all domains.

In 1964, this trend was given official sanction with the Civil Rights Act, which established the principle that certain groups—Blacks, women, and Puerto Ricans, for example—need not abandon their particular identities to enter American society. This marked the beginning of an aggressive new collective-rights orientation in the United States. Following from the Civil Rights Act, tough affirmative-action regulations were passed to guarantee disadvantaged minorities a larger slice of power and influence. The labour force served as the focus for this socio-economic redress, and the goal became participation of minorities in all occupations according to their percentage of the population. Under regulations, all organizations receiving subsidies or government contracts became subject to affirmative-action law with prohibitive fines for non-compliance. As a result of the rise of minority groups in all sectors, the Anglo-Protestant network of power is losing its influence and American society is changing its cultural face.

In the United States, even pluralism in language has made inroads. Federal law, for example, insists that electoral and referendum documents be available in the language of various minorities. The government also encourages social and health agencies to offer services in various languages. This sensitivity to linguistic pluralism was shown in a rather surprising way in the summer of 1979 when a federal court in Michigan decided that Black children in Ann Arbor were disadvantaged because the local school board was not offering instruction in "Black English," the dialect of American Blacks.

Black nationalism and the introduction of laws

and regulations to guarantee the exercise of collective rights in American society preceded Quebec's nationalist groundswell in the late sixties and early seventies. During the Quiet Revolution of the early sixties, Quebecers could see that Blacks were rebelling against their economic conditions and were winning improvements in their status. The American example unconsciously fuelled Quebec's determination to end English domination over the economy of the province.

However, the French were hesitant to accept a vision of themselves as "les Nègres blancs d'Amérique" and did not want to equate their status with Blacks, Puerto Ricans, or women. Before presenting Bill 101, Cultural Development Minister Camille Laurin and his advisers studied American affirmative-action legislation with the idea of adapting it to Quebec. The establishment of language and ethnic quotas in private enterprise could have increased French participation in management of the economy. However, the affirmative-action idea was dropped and the government opted for francization programs in business and restriction of access to English schools. What the government decided to aim for in the economic domain was not the exercise of rights but French control.

Over the past twenty years, there has been a strong tendency in North America to challenge the organization of industry and of the economy in general. The multinational corporations have been criticized as too powerful, too unaccountable, too likely to use resources for their own ends, and too insistent upon reducing everyone to common cultural denominators. The bureaucratization of society—whether through the state or private enterprise—gives people less and less opportunity to exercise individual rights. As a result, more and more of them are defining themselves in terms of group interests. A multitude of different sorts of groups have sprung up.

These range from small tenants' organizations and cultural associations to broad movements to stop the development of nuclear energy. All want society reorganized to reflect certain collective interests.

The anglophone elite of Montreal was slow to become aware of these new social currents spreading through the United States and Canada. More than other English communities, the English of Montreal are attached to traditional forms of social and economic organization and are not very open to a questioning of their values. This is partly because most of the English work in the big-business sector and have not been subjected to the varying occupational, cultural, and ideological experiences of the English elsewhere. Rather than placing the attitudes expressed by certain elements of the French population in a wider North American context, they have treated nationalism as a movement which could be turned back with economic arguments. These cultural blinkers have hindered Quebec anglophones in adapting to the changes that have taken place around them and forging a more creative role for themselves in a Quebec which is mostly French.

On the surface, French society in Quebec seems more equipped to cope with certain contemporary trends. For example, rather than relying strictly upon economics, the provincial administration uses instruments of analysis from political science and sociology. In this respect, it would appear to be more advanced than certain other administrations in North America. In addition, the population is more receptive than others to an organization of society that takes account of considerations that are not strictly economic.

Now that French society is passing from a minority position in Canada to a majority position in Quebec, certain questions arise about its approach in the future to cultural issues. Will Quebec follow the American pluralistic model and make room for cultural minorities? Or will it follow the traditional Canadian model, with the exception that French rather than English will dominate and rights once again will be accorded to individuals but not groups?

Everything would indicate that the defence of French rights in Quebec is simply a prelude to the imposition of French language and culture upon all Quebec citizens. The strategy chosen in Bill 101 clearly shows this. Like the British North America Act, this law is concerned with majority rights and offers virtually no legal protection for cultural minorities. This omission is particularly remarkable given that the anglophone minority accounts for 19 per cent of the Quebec population.

In the preface to the original version of the law, Quebecers were defined simply as francophones. This point of view is also found in the lack of interest shown by the Parti Québécois government in the collective rights of francophones across Canada. Generally speaking, the government favours unilingual entities as do all the other provinces except New Brunswick.

The Language Conflict

Over the past dozen years, language conflicts have dominated Quebec affairs and created an atmosphere of polarization reminiscent of the years preceding the 1837 Rebellion. Deeply imprinted upon the minds of everyone were the comments of Canadian National Railways president Donald Gordon on the incompatibility of French education and English business, the bitter St. Leonard school crisis of 1968, and the movement to make McGill University French. Today there are still disagreements over legislation regulating language use and over preparations to unify the English and French school systems on the Island of Montreal.

Language disputes are not new to Quebec; nevertheless, they did not become the focal point of communal tensions until recently. In the past the main differences between the two groups were social and economic rather than linguistic. English and French coexisted on the same territory with their collective vocations, privileged domains, and ideological perspectives. It was only after 1960, when the French had absorbed the values of industrial urban society, that language became the main characteristic distinguishing the two groups and the central point of conflict.

During the 150 years following the Conquest, language regulations and laws centred upon parliaments and courts. The first indication that language legislation might move into other fields came in 1910 with a Quebec law that forced private communications companies to deal with customers in French as well as English. However, it was not until 1969 and the federal Official Languages Act that a new preoccupation became apparent: the correction of socio-economic disparities between English and French.

Strange as it may seem, it was during the period immediately after the Conquest that language questions were least controversial. The first governor, James Murray, governed in comfortable cooperation with the seigneurs, clergy, and habitants. He considered the Royal Proclamation of 1763, which abrogated the use of French common law, unrealistic and contrary to British interests. More favourable to agricultural settlement than to commercial development, Murray and later Guy Carleton used their influence to re-establish the *Coutume de Paris* with the Quebec Act of 1774. As historian Emile Gosselin noted, during the first twenty years of the colony language and culture were not political problems: "The British authorities did more than use French in their relations with their new subjects. They used French as their own language of work and for correspondence. Nothing gave greater satisfaction to British pride than to be able to show a knowledge of French at least equal to what one would find among the best educated people in French Canada."[1]

After 1780, however, there was a sudden increase in ethnic and linguistic tensions. The British recognized that the future of Canada lay more with commerce than with settlement, so the governors were forced to accept the predominance of English commercial interests over pre-capitalist French society and to favour reform of the legal and land tenure systems. Compromises satisfactory to the two groups might have been worked out, but this possibility vanished with the arrival of thousands of refugees from the American Revolution. These United Empire Loyalists had a long anti-French tradition and they contributed to a rapid deterioration of relations between French and English in the Canadas. Historian Mason Wade in his work on the French Canadians had this to say about the political effects of the Loyalist influx into Quebec:

> The tolerant attitude earlier shown to the French Canadians was replaced after 1793 by a fear of everything French, whether Continental or Canadian. As Britain struggled for its life against revolutionary, republican and imperial France for the next 20 years, an ethnic tension hitherto unknown in Canada was created which left its mark on the French Canadian mind.
>
> The fault lay largely with those Loyalists who had been rewarded for their losses in the United States by offices in Canada. Their fear of everything French, based upon their traditional hatred of French "papists" and their bitter suspicion of French intrigues among the American republicans who had stripped them of their old homes and possessions, became almost hysterical.
>
> They furthered their new careers and feathered their nests by seeing "French emissaries" everywhere and finding "French conspiracies" in the French Canadian efforts to practise the self-government which Pitt and Grenville had granted [with the 1791 Act of the Constitution]....
>
> Their efforts to deprive the French Canadians of the self-government embodied in the constitution of 1791 helped to bring on the Rebellions of 1837-38, for the "unquestioned Democratik Enthusiasm" which they noted with alarm in the 1790s was not to be repressed.[2]

Faced with a more ethnocentric community than before, the colonial administrations slowly shifted their support from the French seigneurs to the English merchants and Loyalists. At that point, language, ethnicity, and ideology meshed in such a way that English and French faced each other in solid blocs.

In their attempt to force the French to accept a commercial society, the English merchants tried to impose use of their language on public affairs. However, the use of one language over the other was not the pre-eminent symbol of English or French power that it is today.

The first real skirmish on the language question occurred after passage of the 1791 Constitutional Act, over the status of English and French in the new Assembly and the choice of speaker. The Act did not deal with the status of the two languages. Until that time, however, the colony's administration and business had been carried out principally in French. The new constitution led to an impassioned three-day debate between the English merchants and the French seigneurs, professionals, and habitants. The leader of the English merchants, John Richardson, said that "making laws to bind British subjects in any other language is illegal, unprecedented, impolitic, subversive of our union with and dependence upon the Mother country," and advocated English-only legislation.[3] Chartier de Lotbinière, who had defended the rights of the French language before the British Parliament when the 1774 Quebec Act was being considered, led the debate from the French side. He said the debate in the British House of Commons leading to the passage of the Constitutional Act revealed the reason for splitting Canada into the Upper and Lower divisions. This, he said, was to ensure to the French "rights to make laws in their own language and according to their customs, precedents, and the present state of their country."[4] Eventually, through a majority-French vote, official status was accorded both languages and a French Canadian won the speaker's post.

Ten years later in 1801 the question of language of schooling appeared for the first time. Through the first Anglican bishop of Quebec, Jacob Mountain, English merchants convinced the governing Executive Council to try to set up an English-only state school system. Until this time French schooling was controlled by the Roman Catholic Church and English schooling was run by the Anglican church and private interests. Neither received government support. Most schools were in the cities and towns, so the French country population was largely illiterate. The idea behind the English state school proposal was to facilitate assimilation of the French population. According to Bishop Mountain, with such a system, "in a few years a new race of men...will be found in the country...and *the surest and most peaceful means will have been found to stimulate industry*, to confirm the loyalty of the people by the gradual introduction of English ideas, customs and sentiments."[5]

In a speech from the throne, Governor Robert Shore Milnes asked the Assembly to consider the project. Milnes was the first anti-French governor in the colony and he openly sided with the English merchants and Loyalists in their attempts to anglicize the French population. The Roman Catholic clergy opposed the bill because they recognized it would lead to conversions to Protestantism. The French-dominated Assembly passed the law, but not before introducing amendments to limit its application. A majority of residents of each parish had to consent before one of these schools could be established, and the independence of the Roman Catholic schools that provided most of French education was guaranteed. For these reasons the Royal Institution for the Advancement of Learning, as the system was called, remained a dead letter. Except in certain English districts, the land grants to set up the schools were never requested.

Without being pushed, however, many French parents sent their children to English schools in Quebec, Trois-Rivières, and Montreal. In his famous report on Lower Canada, Lord Durham in 1839 observed that there were about ten times the number of French children enrolled in English schools as English children enrolled in French ones. "Much as they struggle against it," he wrote, "it is obvious that the process of assimilation to English habits is already commencing. The English language is gaining ground as the language of the rich and of the employers of labour naturally will."[6] This general tendency persisted. Until recently, about 10 per cent of French children attended English schools compared to a negligible percentage of English children in the French system. It was not until the 1960s and the widespread preoccupation with the falling birth rate that this became a political issue.

With the Act of Union in 1840, the language issue became more contentious than ever. Under official policy English was the only language allowed and French lost the status it previously enjoyed. For the first two years of the Assembly, Governor Charles Sydenham showed his lack of sympathy towards French Canadians by naming none to the Executive Council. Sydenham died before English-French hostilities became uncontrollable. Under his successor, Charles Bagot, the French received their full share in the government, but it took longer for French to be recognized as an official language. During a famous debate in 1842, which led to the coalition between Upper Canada's Robert Baldwin and Lower Canada's Louis-Hippolyte Lafontaine, the latter rose and began to speak in French. When one of the Upper Canada ministers demanded that he speak in English, Lafontaine made this reply:

> I am asked to pronounce in another language than my mother tongue the first speech that I have to make in this House. I distrust my ability to speak English. But I must inform the honorable members that even if my knowledge of English were as intimate as my knowledge of French, I should nevertheless make my first speech in the language of my French-Canadian compatriots, if

only to protest against the cruel injustice of the Union Act in trying to proscribe the mother tongue of half the population of Canada. I owe it to my compatriots; I owe it to myself.[7]

After this French was used in the Assembly and the Executive Council, but official authorization came only in 1848 in an amendment to the 1840 Act.

With the alliance of Baldwin and Lafontaine and the implementation of "double majority" government under Lord Elgin, English and French in Canada accepted the idea of partnership and compromise. Within Quebec, however, the juxtaposition of the two groups was different. Rather than creating a true association, the English and French in Quebec agreed that two ideologies, one based on agriculture and the parish and the other rooted in trade and commerce, could peacefully coexist.

Nevertheless, the English in Quebec always considered that the only historically significant society belonged to them. Until the end of the nineteenth century, Montreal was a predominantly English city and the centre of commerce for the entire country. Montreal businessmen of the post-Confederation years were the direct descendants of the merchants who pushed the fur trade to the Northwest and the Pacific coast. These men, who headed railways, steamship operations, pulp and paper companies, and banks, carried with them the conviction that they were part of a vast English industrial capitalist continent while the French were marginal people with no economic, political, or even cultural future.

As in the past, they accepted French society and culture in so far as it did not conflict with economic development and their notions of progress. In the late nineteenth and early twentieth centuries when English industrialists set up plants in small Quebec towns, for example, they expected employees to work on Sundays and insisted that English be the language of work and communication. These attitudes and

practices were a shock to French values and accentuated the ideological barriers which separated
French culture from the English industrial world.

English Canadians behaved this way partly
because they subscribed to the assimilationist views of
the Americans about the waves of immigrants coming
into their country. The predominant culture was
Anglo-Protestant and everyone, whether French,
Polish, Italian, or Ukrainian, was supposed to blend
into it. This English orientation dates back to the
Conquest and was expressed by Lord Durham when
he commented that "the language, the laws, and the
character of the North American Continent are
English and every race but the English... appears
there in a condition of inferiority."[8]

Although a type of biculturalism based on shared
patronage and equality in the cabinet worked under
the initial Union governments, commitment to a
two-language, two-culture state was never established. The idea of two founding peoples was accepted
by the English elites in so far as it allowed a division of
roles and separate domains. In this context,
assimilationist pressures on the French population
were considered fair play and in no way a challenge to
the confederative pact.

Until the governments of Lester Pearson and
Pierre Trudeau, federal MPs and civil servants
strongly resisted any concessions which went beyond
the narrow requirements of the British North America Act. This resistance was shown on a number of
occasions. One telling illustration of English opposition to bilingualism came during a House of Commons
debate in 1927 on a private member's motion to give
preferential treatment to bilingual candidates for the
civil service. Horatio Hocken, the member for Toronto
West Centre and a former Toronto mayor, expressed
a widely held English position when he made this
speech:

It must be plain to anyone who understands English that this is not a bilingual country.... We contend that this proposal is an attack upon English-speaking people of Canada, an attack upon the rights of every English-speaking young man and young woman for it forces them either to learn French or to keep out of the civil service.... Ontario and the other provinces are not aggressive against their sister province of Quebec. It is that certain leaders in Quebec are aggressive against the other provinces, and will not observe the conditions of the act of Confederation.[9]

Henri Bourassa, founder of *Le Devoir* and a federal MP at the time, took in reply a position similar to that of Lester Pearson and Pierre Trudeau when they tried to assure a minimum of bilingualism in the civil service. His words contained a curious mixture of bitterness and hope.

The province of Quebec is not a French province, and the reason why the provincial spirit is still kept up in that province is precisely that attitude of mind, on the part of a certain number of English Canadians who consider Quebec as apart from Confederation just as, for example, some Indian reserves are kept apart for the preservation of the remnants of our aboriginal races. The province of Quebec is one of the nine Canadian provinces. The vast majority of its people speak French, but they grant to the English-speaking minority the right to speak English freely, and they accord them in the local administrations, municipal or provincial, those facilities which we ask in federal affairs, not merely as a matter of right—I would never put the question on that narrow basis—but as a matter of common sense, and true Canadian spirit, so as to spread out into every province of Canada the same spirit of Canadian citizenship which exists in Quebec, and should exist everywhere in the Dominion.[10]

Henri Bourassa's efforts were largely in vain. Though Canada elected French-Canadian prime ministers such as Wilfrid Laurier and Louis Saint-Laurent, these leaders did not dare contest the predominant English ideology and accepted the subordination of minority rights to the majority will. The French language was considered so marginal and unimportant even at the federal level that the French had to campaign vigorously to obtain bilingualism for stamps in 1927, currency in 1936, and cheques in 1962.[11] Simultaneous translation of Commons debates so that French members could speak their own language was introduced only in 1958. Until the 1970s most cabinet ministers were unilingually English, which practically eliminated the use of French at cabinet meetings.

The French in Quebec were deeply disappointed at what they considered to be an English betrayal of the Confederation spirit. Virtual unilingualism at the federal level and abrogation of French rights in Manitoba in 1890 (until 1979), in the Northwest Territories (present-day Saskatchewan and Alberta) in 1892, and in Ontario in 1912 restricted the use of French to Quebec. As a result the French emphasized their differences with the rest of North America and retreated into the protective shelter of a Quebec national identity expressed in terms of "la foi, la race, et la langue."

By the 1960s, however, this isolationist approach had become out-of-date. The Quiet Revolution demonstrated that the values associated with "la foi," for example, had lost their relevance. After World War II, the agricultural parish with its strong clerical presence could no longer serve as the core of French society because of the growth of urban centres and industrialization. The rise of the bureaucratic state and the secularization of institutions in education, health, and welfare also reduced the primacy of religion in communal life. The ecumenical ideas which spread through Quebec during the reign of Pope John XXIII encouraged the clergy to accept these changes. As a result religious faith faded as a national rallying point and became more individualistic and Protestant in style.

The sudden drop in the birth rate and the need to attract non-francophones to the fold also buried the old idea of a Quebec race descended exclusively from the settlers of New France. In 1968, Quebec set up an immigration department and became concerned about how to integrate immigrants into their communities.

The disappearance of "la foi" and "la race" and the myth of the land as distinguishing characteristics left language as the last expression of national identity for French society in Quebec. Because of this, it assumed more significance than it ever had before.

This consciousness of language as a special trademark coincided with a phenomenon which sharpened this awareness. The long apprenticeship of the French population to industrial values gave rise to new economic thinking which encouraged the invasion of the domain traditionally occupied by the English. Following the educational reforms of the 1960s, French university graduates in management started flooding the labour market. Initially they went into the expanding civil service, but by the 1970s this sector was full and they turned for jobs to the English corporate sector.

For the English and French in Montreal, language had become not only the principal point of difference but also the principal point of rivalry. Almost overnight, the language of the national and multinational corporations became an explosive issue.

The St. Leonard crisis of 1968 and 1969 unleashed a linguistic conflict which is far from being resolved. Ostensibly, the conflict was over the tendency of Italian parents to choose English over French schools for their children. The Italian community, however, was simply a scapegoat which served as the object of

French hostility towards English business for the incontestable power it exercised over Quebec society. With this crisis old antagonisms dating back to the early nineteenth century were stirred up.

Eager to calm the English and the immigrants and to keep the economy stable, the government passed Bill 63, giving parents the right to choose the language of schooling for their children. This angered French teachers and intellectuals and contributed to the creation of the Commission of Inquiry on the Position of the French Language and on Language Rights in Quebec. Its report, published in 1972, served as the inspiration for Bill 22 passed by the Robert Bourassa government in 1974.

The language question became so contentious that all discussion on the subject fuelled antagonisms and promoted fewer and fewer possibilities for accommodation. The opposition by anglophones and neo-Quebecers to Bill 22, for example, fanned French nationalism to the point that two years later, after the election of the Parti Québécois, an even more restrictive law was adopted. Bill 101, as it was called, further restricted access to English schools; abolished English as an official language of the legislature and the courts, until the Supreme Court overturned this part in December 1979; proscribed English signs; and toughened francization requirements in business. The demands and resistance of both sides showed that the real issue was imposition of French as the language of the Quebec economy.

Language is such a political issue today that it is difficult for Quebecers to believe that this was not always the case. Over the past two centuries, of course, there was continuing concern in Quebec over the state of the French language by French writers such as Arthur Buies, Jules-Paul Tardivel, and Jean-Marc Léger and by organizations such as La Ligue des Droits du Français, L'Action Nationale, the Sociétés Saint-Jean Baptiste, and La Société du Parler Français au Canada.

But until recently, the preservation of French was directed at maintaining a type of cultural isolation to conserve "la foi" in Protestant North America. Language was not the unique or central issue in French resistance to assimilation. This is why legislation to restrict use of English represents a new approach to the question. For the French, language is now the instrument for communications in all domains, including business, and this attacks the very rationale of the English community.

Until the 1970s, only two bills to promote the status of French in Quebec were introduced. The first, referred to earlier, was presented in 1910 by the well-known French-Canadian nationalist Armand Lavergne. It required public service companies in railways, telegraphs, telephones, and electricity to deal with clients in French as well as English. This law was initially proposed by Lavergne at the federal level in 1908 when he was in the House of Commons in Ottawa. Although Prime Minister Wilfrid Laurier agreed in principle with the bill, he was afraid it would antagonize the companies involved. The Association Catholique de la Jeunesse Canadienne-Française gathered 435,000 signatures for a petition in support of the bill, but the legislation never reached first reading. Disgusted, Lavergne left federal for Quebec politics and presented the law before the provincial assembly. Although the companies involved pressed for amendment, the law was finally adopted in 1911 in its original form.[12]

In 1937, Premier Maurice Duplessis also presented a law to enhance the status of French. Entitled the Law Concerning Interpretation of Laws of the Province, it accorded priority to French in the interpretation of provincial laws and regulations. About this time many French intellectuals, jurists, and politicians felt that the legislative process was becoming too Anglo-Saxon in mentality and that action should be taken to preserve the Frenchness of the political process. This came out strongly at a special congress on the French language in 1937 when more than twenty people denounced the anglicization of Quebec law. Although the law was adopted, it raised such opposition among businessmen, lawyers, and journalists in the English community that Duplessis a year later passed a new law abrogating it. Two reasons were given to explain this about-face. The first was the doubtful constitutionality of the law. The second touched upon the justification for the law in the first place: the poor quality of French in the legislative texts made them unsuitable as a basis for interpretation.[13]

It was not until the late 1960s that Quebec political figures started thinking about the possibility of a systematic program to improve the status of French. The first to become interested in this possibility was Union Nationale Premier Daniel Johnson, who just before he died in 1968 said: "It may be necessary to think about legislating on the use of French exactly as governments have done for other forms of communication." Johnson was probably worried about the fight over immigrant students by the French and English school systems. He had no time to set out a linguistic policy. Nevertheless, he was the first premier to recognize the growing importance that language questions would assume in Quebec.

There is no doubt that the evolution of American society toward pluralism stimulated linguistic nationalism in Quebec and pushed the government to take actions it might not otherwise have contemplated. Bill 22, adopted in 1974, was preceded in the United States by affirmative-action legislation to give minorities such as Blacks, women, and Puerto Ricans more weight in the labour force.

Although affirmation of the French fact owes much to the advent of ethnic and social pluralism in the United States, the internal organization of Quebec society is still influenced by English-Canadian ethnocentric attitudes to language and culture. Bill 101, for example, imitates the assimilationist strategy of the old English elite rather than the new American pluralism. The historic chauvinism of English Canada has been associated with nation-building and the French variety will probably survive until the Quebec majority feels culturally secure. Pluralism, however, is now an important feature of North American culture and its influence is already being felt in English Canada, including English Montreal. The assimilationist policies of the provincial authorities, therefore, risk being strongly contested by different ethnic groups who want their cultures and values and their attempts to be part of the North American economy to be recognized.

The Mediation of the Federal Liberal Party

The most disturbing aspect of Canadian politics during the 1970s has been a strong tendency among French and English voters to align themselves with opposing political parties. Liberals and Conservatives have been moving towards a type of representation which is more and more separate both geographically and linguistically. It therefore becomes increasingly difficult to bring together a national coalition that would produce stable majority government. Divisions of language and culture seem to be eroding the ability of the federal government to govern the country. Twice before in Canadian history has this kind of situation emerged, and each time it contributed to bringing about far-reaching constitutional change: once in the 1830s and again in the decade preceding Confederation in 1867.

Historically it has been the role of the English community of Quebec to bring together the diverse and competing elements of Canadian society and to formulate some national purpose to which all could subscribe. However, the gradual weakening of its economic power and political influence has undermined the historical equilibrium within Canada which has rested on a working understanding between its English and French components.

It was the economic decline of Montreal and the rise of Toronto that deprived Quebec of a large part of the influence it once wielded over the rest of the country, an influence exerted mainly through the

English-speaking business elite of Montreal. This shift conformed to broad North American trends as business and industry migrated from the Atlantic seaboard towards the Great Lakes and the interior of the continent. Two other factors contributed to Quebec's waning influence on the national scene. One was the decline of the old families who had ensured Montreal's prosperity in the nineteenth century. The other was the emergence of the impersonal and bureaucratic capitalism of the large multinational firms.

While the English elites of Montreal were losing the economic leadership of Canada, they were also losing their influence in Quebec. They were no longer able to persuade French voters, political parties, and the provincial government to accept the compromises necessary to maintain a certain harmony within the whole country. From the time of Confederation, this financial and industrial elite had been able to keep historical rivalries under control as long as its presence was perceived by a French majority as vital for the prosperity of the province. However, the decline of Montreal made this kind of mediation impossible.

Throughout most of the twentieth century, the Liberal party was the political forum where the various issues raised by French politicians, English businessmen, Western farmers, and other vested interests were resolved. With Sir Wilfrid Laurier, it had taken over the functions performed since Confederation by the Conservatives under John A. Macdonald, and which had first been conceived by Baldwin and Lafontaine in the Union government. Indications are, however, that its role as the party of national unity may have come to an end.

Among public institutions in Canada, the Liberal party possesses a unique characteristic. It is almost alone in having accepted in its internal operations a practical sharing of power between French and English. In this way, the party has been able to draw support from the two main language groups in Canada and to function effectively as a forum for the arbitration of divergent and competing interests. It succeeded well enough in this role to remain in power for the major part of this century.

This kind of power-sharing does not exist in other national parties. Neither the Conservatives nor the New Democrats, in spite of their goodwill, would find it easy to accommodate within their ranks a sudden influx of representatives from Quebec. They would be hard put to sustain the kind of internal discussions taking place within the Liberal party. Similarly, there would be enormous tensions resulting from any attempt to modify party platforms that have been put together with hardly any French participation at all. The Conservative party, even if it happens to be in power, remains closely identified with regional interests and its members are still far away from a truly national outlook. It will therefore be some time before it can play the role which it played in the nineteenth century and which the Liberals assumed in the present one.

The unique character of the Liberal party stands out even more clearly if it is compared with institutions outside politics. For example, the public service is still very far from the kind of English-French power-sharing that the Liberals have put into effect within their own ranks. Resistance to French participation is quite strong in departments and agencies concerned with economic management, although a somewhat satisfactory equilibrium seems to have been arrived at in those dealing with social and cultural issues. In fact, the federal public service conforms to the traditional stereotypes: the domain of the English is business and trade, and that of the French is culture, social affairs, and politics.

It is in private enterprise, and particularly in the large national corporations, that power-sharing has proved most difficult. The main argument used against French linguistic pressures is the internation-

al status of the English language and its essential role
in the world of business. Even in companies where the
federal government is the sole or the major sharehold-
er, there is little power-sharing. The exclusion of
other linguistic, ethnic, or cultural groups from
executive positions is still very widely practised in
Canadian corporate organizations in industry, finance,
and commerce.

The trade union movement has a strong tendency
to ape the language attitudes of management. During
the 1960s, the idea of using collective bargaining to
promote the use of French on the job was often seen as
a extreme form of nationalism. Canadian and international unions were very slow in providing French
services to their members in Quebec. Only when
threatened by aggressive nationalist raids carried out
by the Quebec-based Confederation of National Trade
Unions did they become more sensitive to the whole
issue of language and to the question of service.
Concern for the grass roots is a fairly recent development in the union movement, where there is a
pronounced tendency for decisions to flow from the
top down.

The role played by the Liberal party during more
than three quarters of a century has really very little
to do with its political doctrine. It was largely
determined by its being the majority party in Canada.
In order to remain in power for any length of time a
political party must take into account the centrifugal
forces at work in the country, and at the same time it
must cause some national purpose to emerge out of the
great diversity of regional interests and sentiments.
The party also must rally a substantial proportion of
the various groups in society: workers, businessmen,
farmers, the wealthy and the poor, the young and the
old, the educated and the unskilled, the progressives
and the reactionaries. It must be attentive to every
group and provide it with the means to be heard.

In its conduct of public affairs, Canada is quite

similar to one-party states where the consensus for effective rule is achieved outside parliamentary institutions such as the House of Commons and the cabinet. It is the product of the party's own political activities: its internal organization, its open-mindedness, the quality of the people it is able to recruit, the nature of the debates it is promoting within its own ranks, and finally its ability to motivate members towards a realistic exercise of power.

The role played by the Liberal party during the first part of the twentieth century was consistent with long-term historical trends in Canada. The English-speaking financial and industrial elites of Montreal worked to perpetuate the economic empire stretching from East to West on which the prosperity of all was said to depend. These people were vitally interested in sustaining the integrative functions assumed by the Liberal party, particularly as they could readily perceive the strength of disruptive regional forces across the country. This explains the keen interest displayed by the business leadership behind the scenes in financing a major portion of the party's activities and in recruiting and promoting some of its political stars.

What the Liberals offered the French population of Quebec was an avenue leading to participation in power at the national level. Energetic and enterprising individuals were given the opportunity to move up the social ladder and acquire a material well-being which might not have been available in other activities. The unshakeable loyalty of Quebec voters to the Liberals was largely due to career opportunities in politics, in the public service, and in the magistrature, which helped compensate for the closed nature of the business world.

Liberal control of the public service and the public treasury allowed them to offer exactly what Louis-Hippolyte Lafontaine had in mind after the repression of the Rebellion of 1837-38: access to government patronage. It allowed the French to overcome their most crippling handicaps—lack of capital and know-how—and their exclusion from any meaningful participation in business life. The patronage system which the Liberals ran according to the varying morality of successive periods enabled the French to increase their collective wealth and allowed the entrepreneurial class to acquire the capital necessary for membership in an industrial society. This way of seeing things survived for quite a long time. In 1960, when the provincial Liberals were investigating the corruption of the previous Duplessis administration, Union Nationale treasurer Gérald Martineau defended his party's actions as having been inspired by "the need to create French-Canadian millionaires."

During the first half of the twentieth century, the open-mindedness of the Liberals, and their easy acceptance of the French, existed in a society very different from today's. French participation in the making of national policies rarely went against existing economic or social interests, as it did after the Quiet Revolution in 1960. The prevailing concept of government policy did not extend very far. Fiscal policies were not designed to smooth out the business cycle or to promote regional development. The power of politicians to arrive at decisions and compromises had not yet been undermined by an army of bureaucrats in full control of information and able to exert a determining influence on public policy.

Nor did French nationalism display the militancy that it suddenly acquired after 1960. Collective goals at that time were concerned with the smooth integration into North American industrial society rather than with the pursuit of a relatively independent national existence. During the first half of the twentieth century, the dominant ideology among the urban and middle-class French favoured the promotion of personal and individual interests within a framework of private enterprise. The English were considered to be more gifted for business and it was upon them that the French were counting for their initiation into the mysteries of economics and technology. It is only after a majority among the French had completely absorbed the values of an urban and industrial society that Quebec nationalism reappeared and began to concern itself with problems of cultural survival.

The political alliance between the French and the English business elites of Montreal, as it came to be realized within the Liberal party, gave Quebec a disproportionate weight in the Canadian federal system. Thanks to the disciplined electoral behaviour of the French and to the bloc of votes they provided in the House of Commons, the business establishment of central Canada was able to retain control of the whole Canadian economy and to steer the country's development in the directions it saw fit. French support from Quebec was instrumental in beating back successive protest movements which arose in Western Canada and which challenged the supremacy of Montreal, and later of Toronto.

In return for the cooperation offered by its political and social leaders, Quebec was offered important economic concessions. Federal authorities maintained fairly high tariff barriers to protect the province's labour-intensive manufacturing industries, such as textiles and leather products, from foreign competition. Similarly, trade policies of the federal government sought preferential access for Quebec's raw materials, semi-processed goods, and agricultural products in foreign markets. Lucrative federal contracts were also made available to struggling French firms as part of the general understanding. Until after the 1960s, nationalism was not an important consideration in Quebec politics, at least with respect to the province's participation in Confederation. Industrialization and jobs seemed more important than collective identity and cultural security.

Financial and industrial leaders in Montreal

firmly believed that if Quebec was to make any economic headway it must modernize its social and cultural institutions. They exerted considerable pressure on provincial authorities to bring about improvements in the educational system, whose deficiencies were held responsible for the economic inferiority of the French and for the unsophisticated character of their industry. Progressive elements among the French concurred in this diagnosis.

During the whole period in which Montreal dominated the economic life of the country, up to the beginning of World War II, it seemed self-evident that French-English relations should be subject to some form of political arbitration. It was quite natural that this should take place within the governing Liberal party. Failure to resolve conflicts and to come up with workable compromises was likely to provoke a crisis which might paralyse the political and economic life of the whole country.

In the past, the Liberal party found it easy to bring together the financial elite of English Canada and the political elite of French Canada. Both were based mostly in Montreal, and they were in close and constant contact with each other. However, since Toronto became the centre of financial and economic activity in Canada, and since head-office operations started their migration westward, the two groups have grown apart both geographically and socially. The gulf between them is too large to be bridged through the agency of a political party and its leaders. Accommodation now becomes infinitely more difficult.

Whereas in the past English and French elites shared some common interest and had to coexist on the same territory, today they seem to belong to two competing societies, bitterly opposed to one another. The Liberal party retains the confidence of the French in Quebec, who see the continuity and the necessity of its role. By making national unity the key point in his platform in successive election campaigns, Prime

Minister Trudeau was simply insisting on the historical mission of the majority party in Canadian politics. But the Liberals have met growing voter resistance in Ontario and the West, where the need for a durable peace with French Quebec is not as evident as it used to be in English Montreal.

The party's effectiveness as a majority party has also been impaired by the emergence of competitors for the power once wielded by politicians and business leaders. With the advent of the welfare state and with the government's deepening involvement in the management of the national economy, the federal bureaucracy has grown to such an extent that it offers a serious challenge to the authority of any party that happens to be in power. It possesses a group mind, and a collective interest that has become an integral part of political processes in this country.

The public service has often stood in the way of accommodations which the Liberal party wished to work out with the French in the interests of national unity. The best-known example is the resistance to the policy of official bilingualism. However, the workings of the so-called merit system of hiring and promoting provide a better illustration of how the public service may frustrate cabinet policy. Since the criteria used in the merit system are generally formulated by English-speaking civil servants already in place, they tend to prevent the access of minority groups to important and well-paying government jobs. The acknowledged discrimination of which women are victims tends to confirm the existence of further discrimination against ethnic, linguistic, and cultural minorities. Political intervention happens to be the principal way in which French-speaking people can overcome biases in hiring policies, and this recourse works to confirm existing stereotypes according to which the French have a great propensity for patronage and corruption.

The expansion of provincial power and the rise of

provincial bureaucracies constitute further limitations on the ability of the Liberal party to negotiate national compromises and to enforce them across the country. With the growing demand for educational and social services, the provinces have assumed a determining role in the shaping of collective attitudes and goals. Thus, their reluctance to give up the unilingual character of the societies within their borders constitutes an almost insurmountable obstacle to a national unity policy such as the one with which the Liberals have been identified. In this respect, the public service in Quebec does not differ from those of other provinces.

The incipient balkanization of the economy and of the political system goes against the very idea of accommodations and compromises such as those which have been the cornerstone of government policy since Confederation. Leadership in Canadian institutions has always exhibited a strong determination and a pronounced paternalism that were instrumental in gaining an acceptance that would not otherwise have been forthcoming. However, the present situation makes arbitration almost impossible because the main elements in the country—cultural, linguistic, economic, and even governmental—are incapable of coming together to dampen the causes of division. The Liberal party is unable to impose itself as a suitable forum for this purpose. It is as if the decline of Montreal as the economic and political centre of Canada had released all the regional sentiments that had been repressed until now in the interests of national unity and of national economic efficiency.

Furthermore, there is now considerable opposition to the notion of economic progress that used to be propounded by the Liberal party and by its allies in business and among the French elites. Bigness and centralization are no longer considered proper answers to current problems. There is a deepening suspicion among small-c conservatives and among left-wing radicals that inflation and resulting social dislocations are the inevitable consequences of big government, big business, technology, and big spending. There is nostalgia for the direct relationships that used to exist in the small towns of the past. Opposition to nuclear energy has become the symbol of the disaffection with traditional economic values. The sophisticated and upwardly mobile individual who tends to attach himself to the Liberal party no longer commands the respect he once did, and there is a growing rejection by the voters of the kind of society he stands for.

The slow disintegration of the complex network of relationships and interests that had helped sustain a certain understanding between English and French for more than a hundred years has undermined the status of the Liberals as the majority party in Canada. As it became apparent that the traditional procedures of arbitration no longer worked, the former government had to seek new ways of keeping the country together, of keeping in touch with what might purport to be the national will, and of hanging on to power. Under Prime Minister Pierre Trudeau, the old conciliatory smoothness and the eagerness for compromise gave way to a new spirit of confrontation. Because the old institutional framework no longer worked effectively, there was a more aggressive assertion of national purpose and more impatience with intellectual opposition.

The various groups that once reconciled their respective interests within the Liberal forum are now too far apart to do so any more; and even if they could, these groups no longer possess the authority to underwrite the kind of political agreements that kept the country going. The French are badly divided among themselves, undecided about their own future and their participation in the federal system. The business community has moved to Toronto and has lost touch with the French, whose disciplined votes in the House of Commons once sustained its hegemony over the country.

As the alliance between business and the French in Quebec was breaking down, Western Canada began to shake off its quasi-colonial dependence on central Canada and to assert its desire for a more balanced and autonomous economic development. The movement, which is strongest in Alberta and British Columbia, indicates that the old political and economic order is coming to an end and that Canada is now entering a new historical period.

The situation is felt with a certain degree of apprehension in Montreal. The city's English-speaking community, once identified with the political and economic leadership of the country, now faces problems of adaptation and even of survival in the new context. The Parti Québécois government and nationalist elements are pressing relentlessly against the use of the English language in management, in commerce, and in public signs. By limiting access to English schools, the government is also limiting the community's ability to replenish its thinning ranks.

However, the most dangerous development for the English community has been the disappearance at the national level and in the other provinces of a policy of compromise with Quebec that would help this minority within a minority to thrive as a group. There seems to be a general acceptance among Canadians of the idea that Quebec should become as French as the other provinces are English, that it too should be allowed to become unilingual. This kind of arrangement apparently satisfies the greatest number while disturbing the fewest.

In any event, it is clear that the concept of a governing party supported by majorities among the French and the English has become unworkable. The era of the democratic one-party state seems to be over. No new government can revive the old formulas for compromise and accommodation, and innovation will be required if Canada is to be made to work again as a economic and social unit.

THE PRESENT

The Anglo-Protestant Ideology and the School System

Nothing contributed so much to persuading the English community in Montreal of the hostility of the French as the repeated attempts of the government to reduce the independence of the Anglo-Protestant school system. Since education is the way cultural values are transmitted from one generation to another, the autonomy of the school system has always been jealously guarded. The community's protective attitude toward the schools is intensified by the close links between the business world and the primary and secondary educational system, capped by McGill University. For the English community, the school system is the training ground for Canadian business and professional leaders. To ensure that the schools are oriented to the community's economic role in Quebec and Canada, the English financial elite has always been involved in school administration, and any blow against the school system is perceived as an attack against the English community itself.

The first signs of worry in the English community about the autonomy of the school system appeared when the Jean Lesage government began its educational reforms in 1960. The creation of a ministry of education was unsettling because it placed education at the centre of political discussion and not on the sidelines where it had been before. The standardization of funding for the Protestant and Catholic—that

is, English and French — school boards also caused
apprehension. But the first measure which was
considered a direct attack on the Anglo-Protestant
educational system was taken in 1969 by the Union
Nationale government under Premier Jean-Jacques
Bertrand. This was a proposed law to reorganize the
various school systems on the Island of Montreal by
region rather than by language and religion.[1]

The objections raised on this occasion by the
Protestant School Board of Greater Montreal showed
the bonds which the community wanted to retain
between education and business and illustrated how it
saw its economic vocation. In a brief about the bill to
the provincial government, the Board stated:

> The economy of Quebec is seriously threatened by
> the failure of Bill 62 to ensure the free and full
> survival of the English language tradition. The
> presence in Quebec of a strong English-speaking
> sector having close ties with the rest of Canada
> and the United States has contributed greatly to
> the economic welfare of all Quebecers. It is vital,
> therefore, not only for English-speaking Quebec-
> ers, but for their French-speaking compatriots as
> well, that in the public educational system,
> adequate provision be made for the curriculum
> and course of study available for the English-
> speaking students to be as similar as possible to
> practices observed in the rest of Canada and
> North America.

The Montreal Board of Trade raised similar
objections to the bill. This association of English-
speaking businessmen talked in its brief about the
important differences between the English and
French of Quebec.

> The attitudes of anglophones are generally better
> adapted to purely economic goals than those of
> francophones into which considerations of another
> order tend to be introduced.... These differences
> stem mainly from education. Consequently, the

educational systems must necessarily differ in certain fundamental aspects such as teaching methods, guiding principles, etc.

It is important to note that in contrast to the French, the English are heavily concentrated in occupations associated with business.[2] Agreement between the positions of the school authorities and the businessmen arises because the community associates its culture with its economic activities and considers survival in Quebec to be dependent upon its control of economic institutions in the private sector.[3] This unity of views, which can be found in other fields such as the church and health services, has been cemented in the past by corporate control of community institutions through the supply of managerial talent and funding.

Legislation on school organization for the Island of Montreal was not adopted by the National Assembly until 1972 and even then parts of it were never implemented. The reason for this was that the English Protestants found unexpected allies among the French Catholics in their fight against government policy. An important segment of the French population did not want to see deconfessionalization of the Catholic school system. They opposed government control of the schools because they wanted to conserve some say over the education of their children. This alliance, which was never official, was able to mobilize personal and private values in opposition to the social and collective interests of the provincial authorities.

The desire of the English community in Montreal to perpetuate its historical role as managers of the economy considerably influenced the school system's attempts to accommodate the growing pressures of the French majority. The type of language configuration which the English envisaged for Quebec showed where their interests lay. During the Quiet Revolution, as the French fact rose in importance, the English community stressed bilingualism as a goal for all Quebecers. Many unilingual anglophones tried to lessen the rapidly rising language tensions by learning French and participating in the French community's cultural activities. They felt, however, that in return the French population should recognize the privileged status of English in the economic domain.

The French opposed the English approach to bilingualism mainly because when it came to making a living, especially in the world of business, the burden of speaking two languages fell principally upon them. This comes out clearly in the Gendron Commission report which shows a small group of unilingual anglophones forcing large numbers of francophones to work in their second language. [4]

The English were never opposed to learning French and this is illustrated by the significant percentages of anglophones who enrol in French courses. [5] What they did resist were the attempts by nationalists to abolish the separate vocations which history and tradition had assigned to the two groups in Quebec. The strong attachment of the English elites of Montreal to the idea of well-defined English and French domains appeared very clearly in a brief presented by the Protestant School Board of Greater Montreal to the Gendron Commission in 1969. "The French Canadian heritage will continue to find expression through the arts, through literature, through the theatre and mores of the people" while the anglophone minority will "assure that Quebec, while remaining forever the heartland of French culture in the Western world, shall at the same time be part of the economic, industrial and cultural life of North America."

This particular concept of a bilingual society, which recognizes the predominance of French and English in their respective domains, is confirmed by many different studies on English attitudes to language use in Quebec. The Gendron Commission, for example, surveyed English workers and discovered that the overwhelming majority thought that all

Quebecers should speak French and that francophones should be able to work in their own language. However, when asked whether they thought French should eventually become Quebec's language of business and finance, fewer than a quarter said yes.[6] Another study showed that the majority of English high school students thought there was no need to improve the situation of French as a working language.[7]

The English community, however, found it arduous to live up to its own definition of bilingualism. For the majority, learning French proved to be extremely difficult, if not impossible. This is because the English middle class congregates in milieus which are socially and economically homogeneous. The English population tends to live in neighbourhoods where French is almost never heard and to work in large corporations where the language of operations is English. This, however, handicaps individuals who need French surroundings to practise what they are learning in classrooms. With few opportunities to practise the language, many gave up their French courses and concluded that English people were afflicted by a mysterious incapacity to master foreign languages.

The widespread inability of English people to learn French had a demoralizing effect on the anglophone community at large, which began to see French demands as more threatening than ever. This powerlessness to deal creatively with a new social situation hardened public opinion on nationalism. Another effect of this failure to learn French was the unconscious decision of the community to shift the burden of bilingualism and accommodation to the shoulders of the generation still in school. Parents wanted to save their children from the difficulties they were experiencing. Consequently, they pressed the school system to rapidly reform its French language programs. Until this time, after eleven years of study, English-speaking children were graduating from high school unable to converse in French. To assure a more practical knowledge of the language, a new program of French immersion classes was opened.

Immersion has now become a permanent feature of the English school system in Montreal and in some respects it compensates for the English community's cultural isolation. At any one time, about a quarter of all anglophone school children in the city are in immersion programs.[8] In the early grades, immersion is almost total and all subjects are taught in French, but as the grades go up, an increasing proportion of the classes are in English. The immersion experiment is now ten years old and the school boards say they are satisfied with the results. In their assessment, immersion programs are producing anglophone children who are fluent in French and able to cope with Quebec society. This pleases the English community, which feels it has found an efficient way of solving its rather embarrassing language deficiencies.

Put to the test, however, the immersion program is not as successful as the school boards and parents would like to believe. Immersion classes are composed entirely of children whose sole contact with the French language comes from their teachers and their school texts. Given the numbers enrolled in each class, experience of the language tends to consist mainly of listening rather than talking. Because of the homogeneity of their social environment, these children have few opportunities to use French in normal settings or to learn about cultural milieus different from their own.

It is not surprising, therefore, that studies of these programs show that students are mediocre in the language and are not penetrating the French society around them. Linguists from the Université de Montréal studied the immersion program of the Baldwin-Cartier School Commission in the west of the Island of Montreal and found that even though students were better in French than students in the regular program, they could not carry on complex conversations and would not be able to take jobs requiring high fluency in the language.[9] They concluded that an English school is not the best milieu to learn French and can serve only as a good starting point. Without daily communication with French-speaking children of their own age, anglophone students cannot make enough progress.

Another study focused upon immersion students in a high school in St. Lambert, on the south shore across from Montreal. It showed that integration of students into the French milieu has been very superficial. "Even with a substantial bilingual preparation, many graduates have trouble making contact with the French world around them," said the authors of the report. Most immersion graduates interviewed said that if they stayed in Quebec, they could eventually join the French work world. Yet fewer than a third felt their French was good enough to attend a French university. More than half said they intended to leave Quebec.[10]

It is clear that the English community showed unusual flexibility in modifying its program of study so quickly and so radically. But the difficulties that students demonstrate in learning French indicate that the English community may be burdening the school system with an impossible mission: that of turning out a bilingual English elite capable of competing with francophone rivals in an economic milieu which will be almost entirely French.

The community's strategy confirms that it wants to convince the French population that it will make up for past sins and learn French, without giving up its historical role. Given the expectations of the French community, however, this accommodation is very limited. For the English, French is simply an additional requirement for the labour force. There is no question of integrating into French society, or even of learning enough about the French milieu to allow anglophones to act as intermediaries between French Quebec and the rest of the continent.

More and more, it appears that the reforms undertaken with so much enthusiasm by the school system will not produce the desired results. English-speaking parents are starting to see this, and the criticism of Education Minister Jacques-Yvan Morin is hastening this realization. Although an improvement over former methods, immersion programs suffer from being placed in exclusively English settings which provide no fruitful contact with French society. What is becoming increasingly evident is that simply knowing French cannot maintain the predominance of the English community in the economic domain which the nationalist French aim to take over.

While school reorganization threatened the independent status of the Anglo-Protestant system, Bills 22 and 101 attacked its potential clientele. Through Bill 22, the Liberal government reserved access to English schools to those who could already show knowledge of English in tests. The Parti Québécois' Bill 101 went much further, and admitted only those with roots in Quebec, that is, children of parents who had themselves attended English schools in the province. These two laws supported a French invasion of the economic domain, and considerably reduced the numbers of children admissible to Anglo-Protestant schools.

The effect of these two laws was to make the immigrant population the focus of a war for customers, so to speak, between the Anglo-Protestant and Anglo-Catholic systems on the one hand, and the French Catholic system on the other. Immigrant children have always made an important contribution to the two anglophone systems. They result in the hiring of more anglophone teachers and in higher government subsidies to the boards. The cost of services offered to the school population is spread over a larger base. At the present time, 25 per cent of the students under the Protestant School Board of Greater Montreal and 75 per cent of those in the English wing of the Montreal Catholic School Commission are of immigrant background.

In addition to laws limiting access to schools, the departure of people whose children would eventually attend English schools is also decimating the English community. The reasons given for these departures include hostility by the French toward the English, the shrinking of professional horizons, and worry about the political situation. These findings were shown in a study on the whereabouts of English young people five years after high school graduation; the study showed that 33 per cent of English-mother-tongue students and 19 per cent of those whose mother tongue is other than English had left Quebec. As the study indicates, the higher the attachment to the English community, the greater the tendency to emigrate elsewhere in Canada.[11]

The first reaction of the English school systems was to defy Bill 101. On the Catholic side, ineligible students were enrolled in English schools with the complete collaboration of principals, teachers, and the union, which accepted the extra teaching load even though it went against the collective agreement. However, immigrant children found themselves in the intolerable situation of being forced to live and study on the margins of the school board without the knowledge of the authorities. As a result, the interest of the immigrants in this sort of solution rapidly dissolved. On the Protestant side, the teachers and the union were less threatened by Bill 101 because there were fewer immigrants in the system, so they refrained from mounting the kind of resistance that would have undermined their collective agreement. The Protestant School Board of Greater Montreal rejected the idea of a clandestine operation and instead openly accepted inadmissible students in the opinion that the public would generously defray the expenses. But when the provincial government threatened to reduce its subsidies, and when it became clear that the public would not help out, the Board abandoned its scheme.

To keep its immigrant population, and at the same time respect the law, the Board came up with a new solution: to expand its small French Protestant sector, which until 1978 consisted of some French elementary schools attached to English schools and one separate French high school. In 1979 a program of "welcoming classes" for immigrant children with little knowledge of French was established, and for the following years the Board projected rapid expansion of classes at all levels. Through this policy, the Anglo-Protestants moved the war for immigrants to new territory.

The Protestant School Board of Greater Montreal is well aware of the attractiveness of its new French system for immigrant families, who view English rather than French as the key to social and economic advancement. The teaching of English in the system would be better than in French Catholic schools, where many educators and students oppose giving a high priority to improving the teaching of English. Second-language learning could be made easier by placing English and French divisions in the same school so the two groups could mix. Without flouting Bill 101, the Protestant School Board of Greater Montreal intends to offer immigrants in its French sector an extensive knowledge of English language and culture which they could not acquire anywhere else.

Another possibility, which the Board does not dare raise at this time, is that its French sector will also attract French Quebecers who want their children to improve their English and to experience a more culturally pluralistic environment than the French Catholic system can currently offer. This would certainly put the Protestant system more in touch with French Quebec culture, but it would also open the door to more direct competition with the various French Catholic boards, whose students are already being drawn away by the expansion of well-subsidized French private schools.

These developments would accelerate the movement to integrate the various school systems on the Island of Montreal, a possibility which the Anglo-Protestants look upon with considerable apprehension. Another hazard is that growth in the number of francophone Quebecers teaching in the Protestant sector would result in a swing away from the English union, the Provincial Association of Protestant Teachers, to the French Centrale de l'enseignement du Québec, whose leftist and nationalist positions are as frightening to the Board as the Parti Québécois' desire for political independence.

What is most troubling for anglophone school authorities, and especially for the multicultural population they serve, is that gradual integration to the majority French society will lead to clashes which will go beyond the recent English-French struggle for position. The fear is that conflicts in mentalities and cultural attitudes will lead French Quebec to reject the pluralism which was won in the United States and which many here would like to see as the replacement for the historic English-French cultural dualism of the past.

Bureaucracy and the End of the Two Solitudes

The English-speaking community of Montreal firmly believes that the steady erosion of its economic power and political influence has been due to the growing influence of French nationalism during the last fifteen years. This is the most widespread opinion in business circles, in cultural institutions, and in the media. It constitutes the most prominent feature of political meetings, and it has moved the English community to try to demonstrate to the French majority how destructive nationalism and separatism could be. There has been, perhaps, a certain awareness that Canadian and North American trends may have spelt the decline of Montreal as a city of finance and industry and that they may have favoured the growth of Toronto as the country's new economic centre. But beyond these elementary considerations, there is very little awareness of the factors that have created the present situation.

One of the most important considerations in this respect is the bureaucratic organization of society and of the economy which has resulted in the emergence of a new class of managers in both capitalist and socialist countries. This class made a rather tardy appearance in Quebec because of the historical dissociation of the provincial government, controlled by a French majority, and the economy, controlled by an English-speak-

ing minority and protected by the federal government. However, the advent of bureaucracy and its
identification with the French majority had dramatic
and unexpected consequences which cannot be identified directly with nationalism.

Nationalism has been the most durable ideological
movement in the history of Quebec. It has been the
favoured medium, as it were, for the expression of
collective goals, in the same way as the business ethic
helped the economic elites of English Canada to
channel popular energies towards the development of
the country. There were periods where nationalism
provided a shelter against the unwelcome pressures of
change, or against the disruptive intrusion of foreign
ways of thinking. This has been the most usual and
most persistent form of nationalism, as for example
during the defence of the seigneurial system in the
early part of the nineteenth century and in the
promotion of the rural parish in the first half of the
twentieth.

But there have been other forms at different
times. They made their appearance in periods of
stress when resistance to change was proving sterile
and when a consensus emerged among French elites
on the necessity of reforming their social institutions.
Nationalism, instead of being directed against the
English, provided the motivation required to overcome the individualism and the sectarianism characteristic of political life in Quebec. In these circumstances, nationalism rides the crest of social
change. This is what took place after 1840 when the
French finally came to terms with capitalism and with
the industrial society of that day.

In 1960 Quebec once more found itself in a
situation where institutional reform could no longer be
postponed. This wave of nationalism was sustained by
the provincial civil service, by the bureaucracy which
needed some deeply rooted cause to consolidate its
power. Its growth was stimulated by a rapid increase

in government spending to meet local and community needs in education, health, and welfare. During a period of more than fifteen years, the provincial bureaucracy became the principal agent of social change in Quebec, outstripping in power and influence more visible organizations such as political parties and the labour movement.

Its main rival was the more powerful and richer federal administration, which for some time had been attempting to impose its control over other levels of government across the country. But the Quebec bureaucracy, because of its identification with nationalism, was able to enjoy a measure of popular support which made the result of its struggle against Ottawa a foregone conclusion. The way was open for provincial centralization of local services and for homogenization of community institutions. This is what put an end to the historical independence of the English community from provincial power.

The bureaucratic confrontation between Quebec and Ottawa took shape after World War II. In order to finance military expenditures, federal authorities had concentrated the country's fiscal resources in their hands. The provinces, by virtue of agreements more or less forced upon them, had to make do with a relatively small proportion of existing taxes on personal and corporate incomes. Ottawa was quite confident that none of them would run the political risk of levying its own taxes, and that it could therefore exert a determining influence on almost every aspect of public administration in the country.

As the fiscal debate seemed to be bogging down in futile argumentation, Premier Maurice Duplessis struck a daring and unexpected blow at his rival in Ottawa, Prime Minister Louis Saint-Laurent. He introduced a bill in the Legislative Assembly calling for a provincial tax on personal and corporate incomes. It was a gesture of defiance, designed to assert the right of the provinces to tax and to spend independently of the federal government. The premier was confident that a majority in Quebec would support him without hesitation. He turned out to be right. Federal authorities were forced to negotiate more generous fiscal arrangements with the provinces. But the underlying constitutional problems were not resolved, nor have they been to this day.

The English-speaking business community of Montreal was profoundly disturbed by Premier Duplessis' coup. It was apprehensive about the long-term consequences of double taxation, as the new fiscal situation came to be known. The most telling criticism was that expansion of provincial powers would contribute to balkanization of the Canadian economy. It was widely held in the years following World War II that the Canadian economy would not be able to measure up to stiff international trade competition without centralized government and a concentration of business decisions. Bigness was thought to be the best means of ensuring continued growth for Canada.

The traditional English view of the French came to the fore once again when a majority of voters appeared eager to pay the premier's new taxes out of patriotic duty. The French, it was believed, constituted a backward society, one that was incapable of grasping economic concepts. To a Protestant business elite it was clear that the power keeping the French in their current state was that of the Catholic Church, which was a highly visible institution in Quebec until about 1960. Only by throwing off the hold of the clergy and by modernizing their educational system could the French expect to participate in the benefits of a modern industrial society.

This judgement, along with the reform proposals associated with it, found a favourable response among a certain French elite that tended to accept the definition of progress put forward by Montreal's English community, by businessmen, and by the federal Liberal party. There was an articulate minori-

ty among the French eager to do away with Premier
Duplessis' government and to overthrow its very
conservative ideology with its pronounced rural and
nationalist biases. The English community found it
very reassuring to witness the growth of a movement
of reform and modernization.

The introduction of public hospital insurance in
1957 aggravated the fiscal confrontation, which had
been dormant for a while. Federal authorities incorporated into the scheme the notion of national standards
whereby the nature and quality of various government services should become uniform across the
country. Their acceptance by the provinces was a
pre-condition for receiving the federal half of the funds
necessary for the plan's operation. Little attempt was
made to discuss these standards with any province, let
alone Quebec. It was all part of a drive launched by
Ottawa towards a more centralized and tightly knit
country. However, Premier Duplessis flatly rejected
the federal proposal, even though taxpayers in his
province would be called upon to help pay for services
offered to other Canadians and from which they would
derive no benefit.

The premier feared that the plan would danger-
ously undermine the autonomy of the province, and
that it might even endanger the continued existence of
a society that was culturally different from the
English-speaking majority in Canada. Moreover, he
was perfectly aware that his administration was
totally unprepared to hold its own against the
bureaucratic monster taking shape in Ottawa. This
was at a time when the first computers were beginning to revolutionize administrative procedures and to
give unprecedented scope to bureaucratic ambitions.
Nor was the provincial government ready to substi-
tute itself for the religious orders that were in charge
of the vast majority of French social and cultural
institutions. This entailed political risks that Duplessis
was not ready to run. His government's refusal of the

federal offer was a desperate decision designed to buy time for a terribly weak and underdeveloped society.

Public hospital insurance finally came to Quebec in 1960, after Premier Duplessis' death and the election of Premier Jean Lesage. Popular needs could no longer be denied. With hospital insurance the government set in motion a whole series of reforms and transformations whose shocks are still very much perceptible today.

Federal regulations called for extremely tight controls over expenditures and over accounting procedures. As it happened, most hospitals were run by religious orders who from the earliest days of the colony had assumed responsibility for education and for the care of the poor and the sick, thanks to money and land grants from the government. The system had worked reasonably well for 300 years. However, its loose administrative structures and its limited resources could no longer cope with the rising demand for health care. State intervention therefore became inevitable.

The advent of the welfare state meant that hospitals had to be incorporated independently of the religious orders that ran them. Every penny received and every penny spent had to be accounted for. The labour provided by the nuns, which had been unpaid, now had to be itemized on payrolls. In many cases, nuns became union members and could occasionally be seen doing duty on picket lines. But the Church had no desire to make a stand against the secularization resulting from increasing reliance on public funds. It was generally accepted that the days of clerical paternalism had finally come to an end. Hospitals were therefore transformed into non-profit organizations and administered along the bureaucratic lines dictated by Ottawa. A similar change later overtook the schools and social aid agencies. Secularization finally came to the labour movement and to the credit unions, which in most instances had been organized under the initiative of the clergy. It amounted to momentous changes in a society that a few years earlier had been denounced for being "priest-ridden."

The initial reaction of Quebec's English community was extremely favourable. It was eager for the free hospital services that were already available to Canadians in other parts of the country. But the most important aspect of the new situation was that the English community had become part of a broad coalition, put together by the provincial Liberals, that included the bulk of the nationalist movement, labour unions, professionals, and intellectuals, as well as businessmen. For a few years there existed a solidarity between the two principal language communities of Quebec that was almost unprecedented in Canadian history.

The reform program which the Liberal government was implementing, usually referred to as the Quiet Revolution, seemed to indicate Quebec's desire to rejoin the Canadian mainstream instead of seeking isolation in antiquated social institutions and ideologies. The economic facts of life received more recognition from the French than at any time previously, and it was expected that the population would rally to the national policies of government centralization and of business concentration. The English-speaking community, and particularly its business leaders, was therefore confident of retaining its pre-eminence and exercising its historical role as mentor of the French, as it were.

This self-serving interpretation, however, overlooked key elements of the situation. The Liberals had certainly not turned their backs on the concept of provincial autonomy. On the contrary, they were deeply concerned with reconciling the notion of autonomy with the various social needs that had remained unrecognized and unmet by the Union Nationale administration. More than any of its predecessors, the Lesage government was determined to resist the continuing expansion of federal authority and its hold on Canadian fiscal resources.

Also unnoticed was the most important development of that period: the emergence of a powerful provincial bureaucracy capable of challenging its federal counterpart for exclusive control over the province's social and economic life. The number of provincial civil servants grew by leaps and bounds, largely in response to the mass of federal regulations that had to be applied as a condition for participating in federal shared-cost programs such as hospital insurance, unemployment assistance, and vocational training. The bureaucracy also grew out of the reforming zeal aimed at modernizing the province's educational system. The expansion of the managerial functions of the Treasury Board helped to consolidate the power of the public service at the expense of the cabinet and Parliament. As the provincial bureaucracy was almost exclusively French and the federal one mostly English, competitition was unavoidable, particularly at a time when all levels of government were indulging in rather giddy spending programs.

The Quebec bureaucracy soon developed a political ideology which, understandably enough, favoured the expansion of its own power. The basic tenet of the new creed was that private and individual interests were to be subordinate to collective goals as defined by technocrats and friendly academics. Nationalist rhetoric was modified to fit in with the new role assumed by the state. The traditional suspicions of the French towards government and authority were completely disarmed by this new class whose integrity seemed to guarantee the permanence of the political reforms in progress. The implied promise was that fickle and corrupt politicians would be kept on a short leash by virtue of this new class's devotion to the common good.

In order to justify the expanding authority of the bureaucracy, nationalism was transformed from a defensive and isolationist attitude into an active movement which could motivate people to accept fundamental changes in the workings of their society. There was a dramatic shift in the long-standing animosity directed at the English, which stemmed from historical events such as the execution of Louis Riel, the abrogation of French school rights in Manitoba and Ontario, and the conscription crises during the two world wars. The federal government itself became the new enemy, the one institution standing in the way of collective liberation. The federal government was an easy target. Federal mandarins, being mostly English-speaking, had little knowledge of Quebec and were prone to serious policy mistakes that could readily be exploited for political gain. The provincial government entered a long period of constitutional guerrilla warfare on a number of topics such as taxation, the rights to spend and to tax, natural resources, the Supreme Court, and communications, all of which contributed immeasurably to the prestige of the new class.

The English community of Montreal was thrown completely off balance by these developments. Right up to 1960, the two language groups in the province ran their respective affairs in parallel and separate ways. Administration and financing of community institutions were largely autonomous. But the growth of bureaucratic empires in the public service soon put an end to the "two solitudes." The expansion of government services and controls, a growing reliance everywhere on public funds, and the rapid rise of public spending have restored to the political realm a whole range of problems and decisions which had been discreetly excluded until then.

The English community had always relied on its business elites for the defence of its interests and its way of life. But after 1960 its community institutions were obliged to submit their policies and their budgets to civil servants in Quebec. It was something of a shock to discover that the informal decision-making of such institutions as McGill University and Royal Victoria Hospital was no longer acceptable. Just like the French Catholic orders, English community institutions had to tighten up their operations and do away with the club-like atmosphere that had prevailed until then. Furthermore, it was no longer possible for community leaders to deal behind the scenes with provincial politicians. They had been frozen out of day-to-day administration by the bureaucrats in the name of efficiency and justice. The bureaucratic spirit, with its unbending objectivity, could not be circumvented.

The English community, particularly its wealthier and more powerful Protestant side, began to experience political disorientation. The traditional way of doing things, with its pragmatism and its informality, could no longer be applied to the management of community institutions. The bureaucrats had to be propitiated with an endless stream of papers and reports. The kind of personality which only a few years before had made for a successful community representative and negotiator suddenly became incapable of dealing effectively with provincial authorities. Painful tensions resulted from the need to replace many of these people with others who could better understand the new administrative procedures.

The most negative, and most important, side-effect of the bureaucratic intrusion was that the business elites who had often lent their talents for the management of community institutions came to be cut off from the rest of the population. The circulation of ideas and attitudes from top to bottom, which had long been a source of strength and cohesion in the community, was interrupted. Consequently, from the very moment they could no longer assume responsibility for community institutions and were cut off from fruitful interaction with their own society, English-speaking businessmen became increasingly inclined to purely economic decisions with a corresponding loss of social concern. This accelerated the movement of head offices from Montreal to Toronto, a movement which seriously reduced employment and career opportunities within the English community. The growing power of the bureaucracy had undermined what loyalty businessmen might otherwise have felt towards their own community.

The social planning and centralized control which became the norm of French society after the Quiet Revolution were so alien to the English community that it saw these developments as basically hostile to its way of life and to its business-oriented culture. For the first time in its existence it became painfully aware that it was no longer in control of its affairs and that it could exert very little influence over the changes that threatened to overwhelm it.

Understandably, the condescension that was formerly displayed towards the French gave way to distrust and to fear. Somehow, they seemed possessed of some mysterious strength that in a few short years had robbed the English community of its power and independence. Tensions rose abruptly in 1967 when René Lévesque broke with the provincial Liberals and made the separatist movement into a powerful political force. The English community in Montreal mobilized in order to fight every manifestation of nationalism, positive or negative, and to bring about its defeat at the polls. But not only did this type of political action prove ineffectual, it contributed to a worsening of the situation.

What proved to be the most damaging attitude of the English community was its extremely narrow definition of democracy as pertaining solely to electoral processes. A very secretive atmosphere prevailed within the administration of most of its publicly financed institutions such as the Protestant School Board of Greater Montreal and the City of Westmount. The elites that had taken charge of them resorted to the same practices as prevailed in the business world. The services provided were very efficient and enlightened; so much so that English hospitals and universities attracted a substantial number of French-speaking people. But the management of these institutions was resolutely authoritarian: it excluded voters and taxpayers at large, service users as well as staff, from any say in policy. It was as if members of the community had become the wards of a business aristocracy. There was a very strong tendency to curtail political debate, to dampen criticism, and to refrain from washing dirty linen in public.

Democratic principles and practice were further weakened by the desire to perpetuate the historical division of labour that had developed towards the end of the eighteenth century in Lower Canada, whereby commerce and industry were the preserve of the English while culture and politics were that of the French. This ethnic division of labour was subsequently extended to the waves of immigrants who were settling in the country. Each new group acted as if it had been given a collective vocation. For example, Jews flocked to the garment industries and Italians went in large numbers to construction and allied trades. Later, however, members of ethnic groups became prisoners of this division of labour and found it very difficult to take advantage of career opportunities in either English or French firms and institutions. The same ethnic hierarchies existed in the rest of Canada and in the United States, but survived longer in Montreal. The end came when the historical agreements that sustained them were challenged by the French elites.

Indeed, there were definite social and economic advantages to be derived from a situation where there is a certain repression of democratic leanings—democracy being understood to include the egalitarian sense which the French of Quebec and most Europeans give to the word and not only in relation to electoral processes. The elitism of the English community in Montreal helped preserve its pre-eminence over the various ethnic groups in the city, and over the French population itself. This would have been more difficult in an open political system.

The English community was powerless to face the bureaucratic invasion originating in the provincial government. The English-speaking population, never having really participated in the management of its community institutions, was not moved to fight on the very grounds where it was being threatened. It was politically illiterate and had little understanding of the basic principles on which it might have made a stand: decentralization and local responsibility. The general reaction was to revert to the traditional rivalries between English and French. This was the kind of confrontation with which everyone was familiar.

Uncomprehendingly and inadvertently, the English-speaking population of Montreal set itself up as the principal obstacle in the achievement of French collective goals. It became a leading target, after the capitalist system, of growing social unrest in Quebec. In such a climate, attitudes quickly hardened on both sides of the linguistic barricades. Compromise became increasingly difficult, particularly in the business world, which aggravated Montreal's economic problems. The moderate nationalism of the Quiet Revolution, which had aimed at institutional reform and at the conquest of a broader economic space, took on with the rise of the Parti Québécois the appearance of a cultural and linguistic crusade, and for certain elements in the party even an ethnic one.

On the eve of the Quebec referendum on sovereignty-association, the only form of political action that will rally a majority of the English-speaking population is with the various national unity groups that have been created for the campaign. This type of political involvement, no matter how legitimate, is very narrowly based and hardly tackles the problems of living in a province undergoing rapid and profound transformations. Its very limited scope points to the demoralization and to the alienation that has gripped the English community since soon after the onset of the Quiet Revolution.

English Business and French Nationalism

Novelist Hugh MacLennan used the phrase "two solitudes" to describe how the French and English communities of Quebec could coexist on the same territory and yet lead parallel but isolated lives. The phrase usually refers to a social situation. However, it may be most pertinent to an economic and business context, for this is where the central issue lies between the two groups, already profoundly divided on the basis of language and culture.

Ever since the Battle of the Plains of Abraham in 1759, there have been two independent economies in the province. One is English. More than 200 years ago it took over the fur trade which the French had launched earlier, and it radiated across the North American continent to the Pacific Ocean. The other economy is French. Because it has always been local in character, it has never had any significance beyond the invisible boundaries of language and of culture. In spite of a growing French stake in commerce and industry, the two economic solitudes have persisted until the present time.

After the election of Liberal Premier Jean Lesage in 1960 and the onset of the so-called Quiet Revolution it became clear the two solitudes could no longer coexist. The French economy of Quebec was called upon to modernize itself and to expand so that it would constitute a solid foundation for the new urban society whose importance was then being recognized. There was also an unmistakable desire to bring all the levers of power in Quebec under the political control of the French majority.

The most obvious target was the federal government, whose powers to tax and spend were deemed to be excessive and detrimental to the harmonious development of Quebec. There were serious objections to the manner in which Ottawa was setting national priorities in such areas as health, welfare, and education. However, lurking below the surface of political agitation throughout that decade was the idea that federal powers were being used primarily to promote the growth of Ontario while Quebec was left with unprofitable industries that had a low technological component and relied heavily on cheap labour. Such a negative view of the workings of the Canadian federation led provincial politicians and technocrats to lay the groundwork for "repatriation" of economic power into the hands of the French majority in Quebec.

The only holdouts among the chorus of praise for the reforms of the Quiet Revolution were the English-speaking business leaders in Montreal. It became clear to them after some time that the political offensive against the fiscal powers of the federal government had little to do with the defensive nationalism of the past. At a time when public spending everywhere was rising giddily, the attitude of the Quebec government could only signal an attempt to obtain the political decentralization of Canada, with its inevitable consequences for the national economy. The business community feared the balkanization of an economy that already had enormous difficulties meeting foreign competition. The fragmentation of political authority, of regulatory powers, and of fiscal policy that went with Quebec's assertive brand of regionalism could only weaken the large national corporations which depended on centralized political decisions.

Suspicions gave way to real misgivings when the

Lesage government sought greater control over the provincial economy. Open hostility greeted René Lévesque, then minister of natural resources, as he campaigned for the nationalization of private power companies. The government was given several warnings not to proceed. These came from financial institutions, which began dumping Quebec bonds on the market. The government, already deep into debt as a result of high spending on education and roads, sought to protect its financial credibility. The only way to do so was to call a general election and obtain a popular mandate to annex the private power companies to Hydro-Quebec.

The election campaign, which was launched in the fall of 1962, was fought on the slogan of "Maîtres chez-nous"—masters in our own house. The government was returned with a large majority. It immediately set out to do what Ontario had done half a century earlier. But the necessary funds did not come from Canada. Banks, insurance companies, and other lending institutions were loath to support such a measure. The provincial government, therefore, resorted to money markets in the United States where its credit rating stood higher.

At that point, the basic outline of the coming conflict between the Quebec government and Canadian business became visible. At issue was the maintenance of the traditional economic order. Provincial politicians and civil servants had already formulated the idea that if the French were to acquire control over the economy it would have to come about from the full use of their collective resources, which meant government initiative and public funds. The first timid step in this direction was the creation of the Société générale de financement.

Another key decision was the refusal to participate in the Canada Pension Plan. A provincial plan was set up and pension contributions levied from payrolls were administered by the Caisse de dépôt et placement. With the huge funds at its disposal, the Caisse de dépôt could seek control of some key industries and at the same time invest in such a way as to promote regional development. The Caisse de dépôt was also expected to invest in provincial bond issues to assist in the financing of government projects. This would give the government some relief from the unwelcome pressures of Canadian lending institutions, which did not approve of the directions public policy seemed to be taking.

Another important step was the creation of a provincial steel company, which was expected to provide a sound basis for future economic growth. The government was already aware in the early 1960s that the industrial expansion of southern Ontario and the rising power of Toronto acted as magnets attracting industries and firms long based in Montreal. There was a desire to respond constructively to this adverse situation. The decline of Montreal was attributable to the growing concentration of economic activity around the Great Lakes in the United States as well as in Canada.

The purchase of DOSCO, the ailing Dominion Steel and Coal Corporation, created the nucleus around which the new Quebec-owned company, Sidbec, could expand. The newly formed company was expected to challenge the unfavourable price structure imposed by the Ontario-based industry. In this context, the involvement of the government in industrial expansion in Quebec was a gesture directed against Ontario and its self-serving control of Canadian development.

In order to provide Sidbec with a captive market, it was intended that all public bodies and institutions relying on public funds would insist on their contractors and suppliers dealing with it. In this way, the concept of provincial protectionism reinforced Quebec's attempts to acquire greater independence from the national economy, whose centre was then in Ontario. The centrifugal forces promoting the balkanization of Canada were already at work.

The reactions of the business establishment were mixed and contradictory. On the positive side, there was a natural tendency to promote more French-speaking people to managerial and executive positions in order to maintain effective contacts with this increasingly powerful and active government in Quebec. By coincidence, these moves helped to meet some of the criticism from nationalist elements about the lack of career opportunities for the French in business. Corporate policies in this respect, however, were largely cosmetic and did not reflect any attempt to revise the basis on which power was shared between the English and French elements of the country.

A more telling and deep-seated reaction to Quebec's regionalism in the early 1960s was the shrinking market for the province's bond issues across Canada. Banks, insurance and trust companies, managers of private pension plans, all displayed reluctance to invest in Quebec government securities. The only way these could be sold in Canada was by paying a marginally higher interest rate. Quebec, even at that time, was perceived as a financial risk which might be included in a portfolio only as a speculative and high-yielding investment. The higher interest rates also reflected the desire of the Canadian financial community to warn the Quebec government that the economic and political course being pursued was not acceptable.

This traditional and discreet method of keeping wayward governments in line helped transform Quebec regionalism into French nationalism. Although the attempts at intimidation were seldom discussed publicly, they eventually alienated key elements among the French middle class. They included people who dealt in securities and who happened to be favourably disposed towards business as well as managers in the public service who could influence public policy. It was driven home to the French middle class that the Canadian financial community would vigorously resist any attempt to alter the direction in which the Quebec economy was developing or to modify its fundamental subordination to the more powerful one in Ontario. In this way, the negative attitudes of the financial community, particularly those of the Bank of Montreal and of A. E. Ames & Co. of Toronto who were handling the province's public borrowings at that time, sowed the seeds of the current confrontation.

In 1966 the Lesage government was defeated at the polls, the consensus being that the Liberals had moved too fast and too ruthlessly to modernize Quebec society and had alarmed voters with their reckless spending programs. The Union Nationale government of Daniel Johnson that followed proved incapable of keeping public spending under control. The premier, unable to come to clear-cut decisions, frightened the business world with his public musings on equality or independence, on the need to regulate language use in the manner of other means of communications, or on the inopportune idea of a political Wall of China around Quebec. His successor, Jean-Jacques Bertrand, was faced with language riots and resolved the problem by proposing a law to guarantee freedom of choice for the language of education and by appointing a commission to inquire into the whole language question. The French population continued to display political restlessness and a growing interest in nationalist projects.

The election of the Liberal party in the spring of 1970 held the promise of stable government. The new premier, Robert Bourassa, campaigned on a program of sound financial management and job creation, thereby demonstrating to the satisfaction of the English community and of business a keen awareness of the economic facts of life. Their view was that demagogy and mismanagement in government were at the source of nationalist sentiment. They believed that an efficient and progressive administration could easily keep the traditional rivalries between French and English under control by promoting a kind of development in which both could share.

This typically English view was shared by Premier Bourassa and a majority in his cabinet when they assumed power: they too thought that economic growth could dissolve social tensions. However, this idyllic view of inter-group relations did not resist the acid test of political power. The massive volume of information available to government officials showed that there was indeed some justification for the collective resentment and anxiety about the future.

It did not take very long for the Bourassa government to complain discreetly about business, particularly the large Canadian corporations with head offices in Montreal. The main grievance was that the firms had done very little to integrate into Quebec society. This was a diplomatic way of saying they discriminated against the French. The point was that they should have been making more extensive use of French suppliers, contractors, professionals, and consultants. But the business networks and contacts on which these firms relied were almost exclusively English and, in a large number of cases, from Ontario. This showed that the French-speaking people who had been promoted to managerial levels had little power of their own, since they had been unable to influence in any appreciable way the direction of their firm's purchases of goods and services.

The premier, who was committed to an ambitious program of job creation, could readily see that a reallocation of purchasing by these national firms would help the province's economy and reduce the number of the unemployed. The ethnocentric attitudes of English-speaking people in Quebec, their belief in the superiority of their cultural group over the French, was perceived by provincial authorities as a real obstacle to the progress of the province. As a rule, English people in Montreal do not patronize French establishments except for fashions, food, and personal services. English reluctance is most noticeable in the broad field of finance: for example, the credit unions in the province have long been more efficient than the banks in consumer loans and they charge lower rates of interest; they have pioneered in inter-branch chequing and in computerized accounts. In spite of this, their customers have remained almost exclusively French. People's private behaviour is naturally carried over into business, where it becomes the institutional norm. Large corporations reflect the biases of the communities of their managerial staff, and this in turn affects the character of their business relations.

Among the French, there has always been a tendency to go along with the negative views entertained about them by the English, who have traditionally been defined as leaders because of their supposed managerial and financial abilities. Hence the French have been prone to patronize English institutions and even to seek employment there as a way of ensuring their own upward mobility in Quebec. Such behaviour has inhibited the development of a modern French business sector capable of competing with the English one, or at least able to hold its own at home.

It was not easy to obtain a meaningful change in corporate policies, principally because they were based on attitudes which were largely unconscious. As with the merit system of appointments and promotions in the public service, the biases of private enterprise are not immediately apparent, except for their ultimate effects. However, the provincial government found itself under considerable pressure to show improvements in this area. The federal commission of inquiry into biculturalism and bilingualism and the provincial one on the status of the French language in Quebec had both contributed to raising nationalist expectations. It became impossible to avoid legislating on language use.

Business leaders were quite apprehensive about the way public opinion was moving, especially because they had little knowledge of the French and few contacts with them. Therefore, when Premier Bourassa launched a round of private soundings on the possible impact of language legislation, he faced an embattled business community. He was told in no uncertain terms that head-office functions and scientific research were out of bounds and were not to be touched: these were two areas where the use of the English language was said to be vital. The premier, who was eager for tangible concessions that would help ward off nationalist pressures on his government, was given little comfort. He was warned that any move interfering with the operations of Canadian corporations would drive head offices out of the province and scare off investors. The premier was therefore forced to choose between nationalism and the economy, as if the two were incompatible. The compromise he chose, or was forced to choose, proved to be his undoing. It also turned out to be a traumatic experience for the English community in Montreal.

The principal justification for Bill 22, as the language legislation came to be known, was the need to counteract the effects of a rapid fall in the French birth rate. It aimed at preserving the numerical advantage of the French by inhibiting the integration of immigrants into the English community. This was done by limiting access to English schools to children who could show a working knowledge of that language. On the other hand, the law was rather lenient regarding the use of French in business.

Government strategy was based on the Liberal conviction that francization of business firms would be realized progressively from the bottom up. It was thought that the gains to be achieved through coercion would be greatly outweighed by the destructive tensions which it would generate. English-speaking businessmen, in spite of their ideological and cultural opposition, were aware of the need to make some concessions to nationalist sentiment. They could also see the irreversible nature of certain historical trends in the province. Therefore, they abstained from criticizing the law too harshly so as not to embarrass the government which, after all, was making a worthwhile effort to improve the economic situation.

The bitterness of public reaction to Bill 22 took Premier Bourassa completely by surprise. He had expected nationalist elements to accuse him of evading the key issue of French cultural survival, but he believed their protests would be outweighed by support from the silent majority. At the same time, he confidently expected that the English community would rise to the occasion and accept in a spirit of realism the adjustments and compromises so clearly necessary for improved relations with the majority in the province. In this respect, the premier had made a serious miscalculation.

It was wrong to assume that acceptance of the government's language legislation by business automatically meant acceptance by the English community as a whole. Yet the miscalculation was perfectly understandable. There had always been a closeness of views between business leaders and the general English public on social and political affairs, not to mention economic matters. However, provincial bureaucracy and centralization had severed the close links which businessmen had long maintained with community institutions. Cut off from their own community, English-speaking businessmen could not warn the premier about the serious risks he was running with his proposed legislation.

Moreover, the large national corporations, with their operations increasingly centred in Toronto, were only too eager to pass the burden of accommodating the French on to the community at large and assume for themselves as little of the costs as they possibly could. In this way the refusal of the business elites to share power with the French in Montreal led them to accept restrictions on access to English schooling which they would never have tolerated at other times and in other circumstances.

The existence of a potential rift between the English community and business did not escape French nationalists. It became clear that as a result of the shift of head offices away from Montreal the English community was powerless to resist the pressures of the French majority. Most of the people with strong nationalist leanings became aware that much more could be gained than the paltry concessions which Premier Bourassa had been able to wrest from the English community. From that point on, the premier was a lost man. There was nothing he could do to recover after being abandoned by moderate nationalist opinion, which went over to the Parti Québécois, and after becoming the target of abuse from the English public and media. After the election of Premier René Lévesque, the consensus in Quebec was that the cultural interests of the French and the economic interests of the English had become irreconcilable.

The alienation of the financial and industrial elites from the English community of Montreal was a gradual process, the most visible aspect of which was the slow displacement of Canada's economic centre from East to West. Already in 1930, Toronto was forging ahead of Montreal as a financial centre, thanks to the industrial growth of southern Ontario. Lack of initiative and weak leadership caused the loss of many opportunities from which Montreal might have benefited, as for example the development of the Abitibi region which was left entirely in the hands of promoters from Toronto during the 1920s and 30s. As the historical role of the city came slowly to an end, so did that of the people who had been closely identified with its economic power.

But the loss of economic and social power experienced by the English community was not fully perceived as such by itself or by others. It retained a certain pre-eminence in Quebec, at least until the Quiet Revolution. Its members gradually became the intermediaries between the French and the corporate decision-makers in Toronto and in the United States. They also retained a near-monopoly of the management jobs available in several industries, particularly those where capital and technology are most important.

No one had foreseen that the decline of Montreal would fundamentally alter the relationship between English and French, particularly the middle classes of each. The most widespread opinion today is that the city's decline is due primarily to nationalist and separatist agitation. For many years now, English political rhetoric has held that Montreal would offer a better climate for investment if the French ceased making unrealistic demands for jobs and remuneration, and for control over the corporate domain of the English. However, if nationalism and the economy must be linked, the real connection must be made in the opposite direction.

In reality, it is the decline of Montreal that has fed nationalism and separatism. The stagnation resulting from the westward migration of economic activity has been causing French opinion leaders to question the links tying Quebec to the rest of Canada, and particularly Ontario. It was inevitable in this context that they would also begin questioning the role of the English community in the management of the provincial economy.

As long as the English of Montreal remained in control of the Canadian economy, their position was secure and unassailable. However, as Montreal's

English-speaking financial elites became the executors of decisions originating outside the province, their situation changed dramatically. By the 1960s these structural transformations in the Canadian economy had become visible. To the French middle class, the English of Montreal no longer seemed creative or possessed of superior knowledge in finance and technology as they had in the nineteenth century and the first half of the twentieth. They simply became unwelcome competitors for corporate jobs, with no other justification for their pre-eminence in the city's business life than their historical achievements.

At this point began the discreet French offensive to carve out a larger and more prestigious place for themselves at the head of national corporations still operating out of Montreal. At the time when Premier Bourassa launched his ill-fated consultations preliminary to Bill 22, the vast majority of French-speaking people in Quebec were convinced that the economy of the province would eventually be managed entirely in French. The problem, as most people saw it, was to avoid a transition that was too abrupt.

The decline of the city of Montreal and of the English community also had a significant impact on federal politics. The Liberals, Conservatives, and New Democrats all came around to the view that Quebec should become as French as Ontario was English. This represented a considerable shift away from the spirit of the British North America Act, which has accorded special protection to the English-speaking and Protestant minority in Quebec. Opposition in the Western provinces to Prime Minister Trudeau's policies on bilingualism also served to reinforce the notion of Quebec's Frenchness, as opposed to the Englishness of the rest of Canada.

What emerged was a new vision of Canada: a country composed of two unilingual parts, one English and the other French. Provincial governments across the country had a strong interest in promoting this kind of vision. They were not eager to assume the administrative responsibility and the financial burden of providing a full range of bilingual services in education, health, welfare, and other areas.

In this way, Montreal's English-speaking community was deprived of any sympathy from outside Quebec and was therefore in almost complete political isolation. The election of the Parti Québécois in 1976 brought about a heightening of the pressures on the use of the English language, in education, in advertising, and in the internal and external communications of private enterprise. Premier Lévesque, who admitted to some embarrassment at certain oppressive aspects of Bill 101, proposed to the other provincial premiers a reciprocal broadening of linguistic rights. But they self-righteously refused to have anything to do with such a deal. Whatever doubts may have existed at the time of the Parti Québécois' election about linguistic trends in the province were quickly dispelled. The only questions that remained unanswered were the duration of the transition towards French unilingualism and the size of the English-speaking community that would remain.

Large national corporations did not sit back and wait for the answers. The anticipated shortages of English-language professionals and executives in Montreal, and the resulting absence of adequate supporting services, have practically forced head offices to move many of their key operations out of Montreal, leaving behind only those services and departments specifically related to their Quebec market. Some companies have left behind only a symbolic head office. Others, like the Royal Trust, transformed themselves into subsidiaries of newly incorporated federal companies which were designed to take over all their business except what pertained to Quebec. Others still, like Sun Life, pulled out noisily, destroying for the sake of a political splash a large part of the business that had been built up carefully over the years. For most companies, the move out of the province has been quiet and piecemeal, except for frequent references to the losses which Quebec must sustain because of nationalism.

The two economic solitudes which used to exist on the same territory are now pulling apart geographically. Increasingly, Quebec is conceded to be a French economic territory where the use of English is reserved for communications with the outside. The French, who think principally in political terms, see this trend as one that will strengthen their control over their own society and eventually ensure a more balanced economic development. The English, who are economically minded, believe the opposite will take place: that by detaching itself from the national economy Quebec will grow weaker and will court disaster.

During the transition period that is serving as a prelude to the disengagement of French and English Canada, the Quebec economy retains the dualism it has displayed since the onset of the Quiet Revolution. One part of the economy is in the hands of French collective institutions: the provincial government and its agencies, Crown corporations and mixed companies with public and private capital, and the powerful credit union movement. The other part of the economy is represented by the large national corporations who are setting up their Quebec business as semi-independent operations in French hands. For the time being there is some rivalry and hostility between the two groups, whose loyalties and antecedents are very different. One springs from a collective will to control the economy for purposes that can be identified with nationalism, while the other group is made up of the successors of the departing English managers and executives who retain their business-oriented ideology.

It can be expected that, as time goes by, these

two antagonistic camps will be coming closer together. This will happen as the French managers of the national and multinational corporations in Montreal establish their own networks of suppliers, consultants, and contractors. There will be a growing tendency for these Quebec subsidiaries to assert their independence from the Canadian head office, particularly as cultural differences begin to show themselves in managerial practices and attitudes.

This new situation could easily constitute the basis for the next crisis in Quebec's stormy relations with the rest of Canada. For at that moment, Quebec will have achieved something unprecedented in its history: a new-found unity resulting from the fusion of society and of the economy which in the past had been the opposing poles around which French and English had rallied.

The English Media and Group Anxiety

The written press, television, and radio are often said to have an educational role to perform and they are expected to act in such a way as to reinforce democratic traditions. In this light one would expect them to lead the way in helping the English-speaking population of Montreal come to terms with the French majority and explore various avenues of accommodation. They seem to be doing exactly the opposite, contributing to an increase in collective anxiety and to a sense of isolation and powerlessness. In fact, until recently the English media's approach to events in Quebec has been so negative as to encourage the exodus of their own audiences. The militancy that has developed on all issues surrounding the historical and constitutional rights of the English population tends to antagonize the French and to strengthen the influence of the more nationalist and aggressive elements.

Trends that have appeared during the last two decades have robbed the media of their capacity to lead opinion as they did in earlier days. Instead, they have become reflectors, or even amplifiers, of the public mood. It is now practically impossible for newspapers dependent on mass circulation and on advertising to express viewpoints that are consistently opposed to those held by the readers. However, it would be wrong to believe that advertisers or powerful economic interests are exerting a sinister influence on media contents to make them consistently critical of the political goals of the French majority in Quebec.

The explanation is simply that news and advertising have become part of a single information
package that caters to the image that readers have of
themselves, of their goals in life, and of the social
environment in which they would like to live. The days
when newspapers were the objective chroniclers of
officialdom have long passed. Only a minority of
subscribers read mainly for knowledge of political
processes and business trends, of events in faraway
countries and the statements of prominent people.

Most readers of mass-circulation newspapers
want the illusion of a world theatre where politics and
consumerism tend to blend with each other. They scan
the contents in order to assess their place in society
and to discover some clues that will suggest how they
should think and behave. They expect newspapers to
reinforce their vision of the world, not to challenge it.
In these circumstances, advertising is not only a
complement to the news. It becomes information
itself. It makes everything inviting by introducing
fashions, entertainments, and a wide range of products
and activities that will give readers the impression
that they live in a dynamic and interesting society.
Advertising is more than commercial promotion; it is
the description of a state of material well-being and
leisure which for most people represents a social
norm. Accordingly, advertising cannot be dissociated
from the other elements that go into a newspaper,
such as political and sports news, editorials, the
business pages, comics, and various columnists.

The English-speaking population of Montreal
possesses unique characteristics that make it an ideal
target group for ad agencies and media. The Anglo-
Protestant group, which is still dominant in the
management of large financial and industrial firms, is
considered to be the most affluent and best-educated
group in the country. It is a highly prized advertising
market. Its economic pre-eminence and its material
achievements constitute a model for other groups in

Quebec such as Jews, various ethnic communities, newly arrived immigrants, and even a substantial part of the French population. The English are seen as having realized the goals of all those who are personally ambitious and upwardly mobile.

English language media will therefore present information, both news and advertising, in such a way as to support the social attitudes and the life styles of the dominant group. Readers and viewers should not be disturbed beyond certain reasonable limits by the presentation of the news. This approach, which commercial interest imposes on the media, seriously limits the scope of any public discussion on important local issues. It also stands in the way of a more realistic assessment of the English community's economic rivals, who now enjoy the very active support of the provincial government.

Capacity for change is hampered by the absence of a tradition of open administration in English community institutions such as hospitals, schools, and universities. The character of the national economy, particularly its promotional and speculative side, encouraged clannishness and secrecy, and these attitudes were carried over into the administration of community institutions to which business leaders were lending their talents. The collective behaviour of Montreal's English population, therefore, has always tended to suppress controversy and to reject internal criticism as a product of extremism or eccentricity.

French society in Quebec, with its very long tradition of clericalism, exhibits the same authoritarian streak. But the difference is that it is more difficult to marginalize internal opposition and to drive it underground. The spirit of French politics is much too adversarial for that. Furthermore, opposition can easily survive in various political sanctuaries. The best example is Radio-Canada during the 1950s under the tyrannical rule of Premier Duplessis. The English community itself constitutes another such sanctuary whenever French internal politics become too oppressive.

English journalism in Quebec is very much preoccupied with events and displays little interest in their causes. It is static rather than dynamic, and it is fearful of social change. It will insist on the threat of French nationalism but will not be inclined to explore ways of countering some of its more negative effects. Its fear of change and its somewhat negative views on adjustment cause the English media to be the spokesmen of a business elite which has already turned its back on Montreal.

Public indifference to Quebec politics, except for the more lurid aspects of nationalism, has a detrimental effect on the quality of journalism. Right up to 1960, Quebec politics was looked upon as something that concerned solely the French and was of little interest to anyone else. Until then, local and community institutions had little to do with provincial authorities and remained relatively autonomous. Business problems were never aired publicly but resolved behind the scenes with provincial politicians. The federal government was felt to be the real centre of power where the most important decisions originated. This perception survived the Quiet Revolution and the dramatic increase in provincial authority and initiative. Although their provincial taxes were growing by leaps and bounds, and although a reformist and bureaucratic administration was smothering local responsibility, most English-speaking people could not imagine that provincial politics could be either interesting or important.

This attitude had its roots in Confederation itself. The constitutional arrangements of 1867 were designed to satisfy two basic requirements of British America. The first was the necessity of granting the French some measure of control over their own affairs. The second was the desire to place important economic decisions beyond the reach of a French veto power and under the control of an English parliamentary majority. The neat division of power between federal and provincial jurisdiction embodied in the British North America Act has remained ingrained in the English mentality in Quebec until fairly recently, and even today still exerts a strong influence on political attitudes.

Faced with the resistance of their public, English media in Montreal find it difficult to present a balanced coverage of events in Quebec and of trends in the French community. It is not always possible to hold back feelings of animosity and even hostility. This tends to keep political thought within the narrow confines of an anti-nationalist struggle.

There exists a deep historical memory of French resistance to progress and of attempts made on several occasions to sabotage it. Today, there is a deep concern about the effect of nationalism on business, a domain over which English Montreal feels certain proprietary rights. The exodus of head-office functions from the province, which is undermining the viability of the English community, is causing many of its members to reassess their personal future, something which is not easy in times of social tension.

Alienation is a sentiment that any population finds extremely difficult to convey. The community links which Anglo-Protestant institutions used to sustain have weakened under bureaucratic encroachments. The blind resistance to every real or imagined threat stemming from French nationalism is inspired by alienation, and this resistance serves to mask feelings of powerlessness and of isolation which are not allowed to surface. These are the complex feelings which the English-language media are trying to express as best they can, according to the hopes and fears of their reading, listening, and viewing publics.

If media audiences constitute a powerful limiting factor on the exploration of social and political issues in depth, there are also factors peculiar to the English

Quebec media themselves which keep discussions within narrow and predictable channels. These have to do with the character of management and with the objectives being pursued. In this respect, the English-language press in Montreal—the *Gazette* and the now-defunct *Star*—is particularly instructive in the way it set out to reflect its readership's self-image and ability to react to an outside challenge.

Both dailies became the property of national newspaper chains in recent years, the *Gazette* becoming part of Southam Newspapers in 1968 and the *Star* of FP Publications in 1973. Previously they had been in the hands of prominent Montreal families who had gradually lost the interest and the will to continue. Economic and social pressures had robbed publishing of a great deal of its prestige, influence, and profits. The families also were unable, by themselves, to tap the managerial talent and the financial backing to keep the two newspapers afloat. This is why they were eventually sold to national corporations whose business was marketing information. It was a decision which confirmed the growing weakness of Montreal's financial leaders. Ostensibly, the change in ownership had little effect on day-to-day operations, and though each newspaper was allowed to arrive at its own decisions without interference from head office, some extremely important transformations took place almost unnoticed.

For a long time the two newspapers had been an integral part of the complex power network that had dominated national life until the decline of Montreal cut off the city's English-speaking population from its former influence on national and provincial affairs. The takeovers by Southam and by FP Publications took place at a time when this situation became visible. They coincided with the movement of head offices out of Montreal and with the transformation of Quebec's economic activity into subsidiary and branch-plant operations that increasingly tended to be handed over to a new French managerial class.

Inevitably, the two English-language newspapers gave up their close identification with vested interests in finance, industry, and politics. They resolutely turned to the marketing of information, that is, of news and advertising. This meant, of course, that the old-fashioned and not entirely realistic view of the press as educator and opinion leader had finally become obsolete. These changes had been under way for some time, but the advent of the newspaper chains in Quebec helped to accelerate and complete the process. Subsequently, the commercially oriented spirit of the two chains brought the two newspapers closer to the general attitudes of their readers. Instead of leading and shepherding public opinion as they had done before, they began catering to their respective readerships, as newspapers in other parts of Canada and in the United States had already been doing for some time.

The new situation naturally called for new forms of journalism. Instead of being at the ideological service of a business elite, the two publishers offered products that sought to satisfy the largest number of customers. This was done by maintaining a certain variety of subject matter and of tone, and by seeking to be interesting rather than merely informative. Accordingly, there has been a tendency to magazine-like presentation, with plenty of columns and features, obtained cheaply from U.S. publications.

This type of journalism assumes that news will be selected not according to its historical or objective significance but according to its anticipated impact on different categories of readers. Depending on the temper of the times, news reports will be attuned to the anxieties of certain groups of people, to their desire for cheer and entertainment, to their propensity to share in the experience of others, and occasionally to give satisfaction to their prurient instincts.

Presentation aims at producing an emotional response from passive readers, to provide them with the illusion that they participate in a broader and livelier society than the one they are personally moving in.

Therefore, the most important consideration for managers and editors at the *Gazette*, and previously at the *Star*, has been an understanding of their potential audience rather than familiarity with the subject matter being reported on. In relatively homogeneous cities such as Toronto and Vancouver, the two may actually overlap: to know the newspaper's readership is to know what is going on. But in Montreal the situation is very different. A large proportion of the news published in an English daily originates outside the English community and deals with people with whom they have little cultural affinity. City Hall as well as the provincial government are almost exclusively French. Thus, in recruiting managers, the principal consideration of the English-language press has been to find people who will identify with the social and political attitudes of the English population. Knowledge of Quebec and of its institutions remains a very secondary consideration.

There is no other way of accounting for the fact that the vast majority of managers and editors at the *Gazette* and the *Star* could never speak a word of French, and had at best only a sketchy knowledge of the province and of the French majority that has turned out to be so threatening. Their field of expertise has been the presentation of the product offered to the readers rather than news gathering. These people have been exponents of what might be called formula journalism, of which the *Toronto Star* has been the most successful practitioner in this country.

French mass-circulation papers have undergone the same transition from ideology to commercialism. In this case, however, the trend has been vigorously opposed by the reporters and their unions. Several strikes have already been waged on this particular issue, but without much success. The bitterest one closed down *Le Soleil* in Quebec City for ten months in 1977 and 1978. Reporters were asking for co-management rights in the newsroom and for a veto over news presentation.

The union's demands on this occasion were couched in rather radical terms and they amounted to a denunciation of consumerism, capitalism, and economic liberalism. But the union's goals were essentially conservative: it wanted to maintain the pre-eminence of intellectuals in French society and to push aside whatever rivals might emerge on the coattails of commercialism and marketing. The strike at *Le Soleil* is therefore consistent with historical trends in Quebec whereby professionals and intellectuals have sought a monopolistic power to determine the goals of their society.

Though the practices and composition of English newspapers may satisfy the requirements of the industry and of the reading public, they impede the English community's ability to take stock of what is actually happening in the province and to react constructively to the undoubted challenge of French nationalism. Two unfortunate effects of news and editorial policies applied under Southam and FP ownership have been to deepen the isolation of the English community and to antagonize nationalist elements among the French.

Managerial inability to speak French, coupled with the lack of contact which this implies, must inevitably influence the assignments given to reporters, the way their copy is edited, and the selection of material for publication. Editorial views may also be affected. A unilingual management and editorial staff are highly unlikely to insist on the necessity of making bilingualism a job requirement in some English institutions and companies, nor are they likely to engage in public debates that might raise awkward questions about their personal qualifications. In fact, the tendency has been to fall back on arguments promoting the use of English as the international language of business, technology, and diplomacy. In the same vein, the French are often reproached with shortsightedness in refusing to acknowledge the superior status of the English language in these very fields.

These attitudes on language tend to create certain staff problems. Reporters must necessarily be bilingual if they are to report on politics and on most subjects of general interest. As a result of their daily contacts with the French, most have acquired a fairly good knowledge of Quebec society. They are not as likely to perceive it as a hostile environment as are the unilingual managers of the media and of large Canadian corporations. Consequently, as a result of numerous persistent disagreements on various aspects of journalism, from assignments to editing, morale and initiative on these papers were never very high in recent years.

Managerial inability to adapt to changing social and political conditions, in addition to the paternalistic traditions of the English community's leadership, contributed to the shipwreck of the *Montreal Star* in September 1979. Its immediate cause was an eight-month pressmen's strike which had started in the preceding year and which had driven away both readers and advertisers. But the strike was only a symptom of an unhealthy climate which pushed employees and unions to formulate claims that might have been excessive, and which drew management away from the promotion of quality that could have ensured greater reader loyalty.

Ever since the election of the Parti Québécois in 1976, there has been an obsessive concern over the prospect of the referendum on sovereignty-association. Everything that has a bearing on the campaign is presented as if a gigantic debate was being conducted with the French-speaking population on the respective merits of federalism and of separatism. However, the range of news and commentary offered the readers has tended to encourage confrontation with the French rather than compromise.

A significant example is coverage of Bill 101, which restricts access to English-language education. The law's contents have been constantly illustrated by means of interviews and feature articles calculated to bring out its most vexatious and oppressive aspects. The people presented in human-interest stories are usually those who represent the most unfortunate situations arising out of government action or who express the most extreme viewpoints on its general aspects. The cumulative effect of these stories is to reinforce English stereotypes about the French. Quebec emerges as an oppressive and inhospitable society, dominated by a group of fanatics eager to destroy personal rights and democracy.

This polemical use of information also contributes by inference to reviving Lord Durham's adverse judgement that the French were unsuited for the conduct of commerce and industry. There has been a steady stream of articles dealing with the negative effects of nationalism on the provincial economy. They often contain allusions to the historical English role in building Quebec's industry and warnings that persecution will drive them out of the province with their skills, their capital, and their jobs. The numerous restrictions on the use of English, particularly at the management level in private enterprise, are said to be leading the French to isolation from the progressive world of business and condemning them to stagnation and backwardness. The indispensability of the English is constantly coupled with the dependence of the French.

This form of journalism soon becomes mindless and repetitive. Little by little, it destroys the capacity to assess situations and trends with realism. It depletes the fund of knowledge that exists in any newsroom and that is shared among a large number of reporters. It prevents newspapers and other media from reacting in a healthy way to unexpected and threatening events such as the election of the Parti Québécois. More seriously, it maintains the English-speaking population in a state of powerlessness in the face of unwelcome pressures and it prevents a positive adaptation to French expansionism.

PERSPECTIVES
FOR THE
FUTURE

Rivalry over the Ethnic Minorities

Like most large North American cities, Montreal has been profoundly marked by waves of immigrants whose cultures, life styles, and ambitions have shaped the metropolis. Park Avenue could be a slice of Piraeus with its tavernas smelling of squid and retsina wine and its corner groceries lined with barrels of Greek olives. Further north around the Jean Talon farmers' market, black-shawled grandmothers chatter in Sicilian dialect, men gather to talk in espresso bars, and women carefully tend tiny gardens brimming with exotic produce. To the south around the intersection of Coloniale and Prince Arthur Streets, old houses painted in pastel colours and decorated with flower boxes and ceramic religious images recall villages of the Azores. The presence of foreign communities is visible in other parts of the city: Haitians around Bélanger Street, Vietnamese in the Cote des Neiges area, Indians near Snowdon, each of them creating a distinctive atmosphere which helps them to feel at home.

The flow of immigrants has changed considerably over the years. Up to the end of World War II, Britons, Jews from Eastern Europe, Germans, Ukrainians, Poles, Scandinavians, and a first wave of Italians predominated. New groups, Italians, Greeks, and Portuguese, arrived during the period of economic expansion after the war. Later, as a result of changes in Canadian immigration policy, it became the turn of Asians, West Indians, and Latin Americans.

The immigrants who arrived in Quebec tended to integrate into the English community, mainly because English was the language of the economy and it exercised a strong pull on individuals who had left their countries of origin for economic reasons. French society did not seem interested in opening up to foreigners. But the fall in the birth rate among the French threatened to disrupt the demographic equilibrium in Canada and to undermine the political leverage of the French of Quebec.

As a result, the provincial authorities pressed the federal government to take account of demographic shifts in Quebec and to facilitate entry of immigrants who were "francophonisable." At the same time, the Quebec government began programs to help immigrants integrate into French life and to inhibit their immersion into the English milieu. Finally, through laws on education—Bill 22 and Bill 101—they tried to divert newcomers from the English to the French community. It was at this point that about half a million people became the key issue in the English-French conflict.

By the summer of 1978, the anglophone elite was beginning to understand the dimensions of the conflict and the consequences of the legislation on its community institutions. A year earlier, the Protestant School Board of Greater Montreal decided to defy Bill 101 and allow immigrants into its schools. By 1978, however, it was clear that an open revolt could not continue and that the Board would have to obey the law, resigning itself to the loss of the immigrants and an eventual massive drop in enrolment.

Bill 101 evoked different reactions from immigrants, particularly Greeks and Italians, who were the most numerous minority groups in English schools. These people came to Canada to escape economic stagnation in their countries of origin and to find prosperity. Although they knew they might have to stay in jobs in factories, maintenance, and restaurants, they were confident that they could propel their children into a higher socio-economic class. To assure the greatest possible social mobility for their families in Quebec and in Canada, they wanted to enrol their children in English schools. It was this avenue that Bill 101 was blocking off.

The vital interests of these two groups forged an unusual alliance between Anglo-Protestant businessmen and educators with their Anglo-Saxon politeness and reserve, on the one hand, and semi-literate blue-collar Sicilian and Greek workers with their capacity for Mediterranean indignation, on the other. This alliance had first taken shape ten years earlier during the St. Léonard school crisis, when a Catholic school board in the northeast of the city decided to phase out English schools for the Italian population. The Italians looked for allies against French nationalists and found them among the Anglo-Protestants who were also starting to feel threatened. It was this community of interests which persuaded the commissioners of the Protestant School Board of Greater Montreal to disobey parts of Bill 101 for the 1977-78 school year.

By the summer of 1978, however, the alliance was showing signs of strain. The English community always portrayed its defence of the immigrants' right to English schooling as support for individual rights, and in the beginning the immigrants felt this approach was sincere. But as English-French tensions increased, and as it became clear that the immigrants were at the centre of the conflict, they began to perceive the situation differently.

The views of the immigrants were summed up during a tense meeting of the Protestant board when the commissioners were re-evaluating their decision of the year before on Bill 101. The head of the Greek community told the Board that the Greeks were tired of being treated as pawns of the English establishment in its fight against French nationalism. Because of their links with the English, Greeks and other immigrant groups were becoming the target of French hostilities. The Greek spokesman accused the English of using this situation to their advantage. He added that although the Greeks wanted English schooling for their children, they were not hostile to the French and intended to remain as neutral as possible in the circumstances. The school commissioners were surprised at this outburst. "Why would they think we were using them as pawns?" asked Board president Joan Dougherty. "For us, support for immigrant access to English schooling has always been a question of civil liberties... of individual rights."

This political awareness among the new Canadians of Montreal does not stop there. The "Québécois de nouvelle souche" ("Quebecers of new origin"), as they are now called by the provincial government, know very well that they are a third political force that can refuse to be manipulated like a computer-program variable to raise or lower the weight of the English and French school sectors. They are now numerous enough to disturb the functioning of any institution which does not take their aspirations into account.

In the past, the anglophone community did not worry about currying the favour of the ethnic minorities and took their presence for granted. Today, however, the ethnic minorities are essential for its cultural and political survival. Anglo-Protestants are tending to leave the province, while members of the minorities, who are more fluent in French and more willing to accept the demands of French society, are tending to stay. This is why immigrants are so important for the survival of English community institutions such as hospitals, universities, colleges, and social services.

For the French community, the immigrants are important for long-term demographic reasons and this puts them in direct competition with the English community. If the French are to win over the immigrants, however, they must try to arrange an integration that allows the newcomers freedom to pursue their own interests. What is likely to disturb relations between the French and the ethnic groups is the conviction among the minorities that English is the language of advancement and French the language of marginalization.

It is important to understand that newcomers to Quebec have no particular loyalty to either of the language communities. Integration is a slow process that can take two or three generations depending upon the culture of origin. Even children born here often feel more Italian, Greek, or Portuguese, for example, than Canadian or Québécois. In their new country, immigrants identify more with North America than with the limited area of Quebec. They would like to speak both English and French, but tend to prefer English. The newcomers, however, want to stay in the good books of both language communities and so they try to strike a balance that will serve both their economic interests and their social integration.

The behaviour of the minorities is in large part governed by their conviction that Quebec society is marginal in North America, not simply in language and culture, but also economically. The French community does not attract them, and in the circumstances, the source of its rising power seems inexplicable. The English community, by contrast, seems strongly connected to the economic life and organization of the country.

As in other large cities in Canada and the United States, the English in Montreal established an ethnic pyramid of power with Anglo-Protestants (surrounded by Irish, Germans, and Scandinavians) at the top, Jews in the middle, Slavs and Mediterranean peoples further down, and Blacks at the bottom. The ethnic groups have always felt ambivalent about this system. They liked the security which they found in their linguistic and cultural "ghettos" or communities, but they complained of being poorly received by the Anglo-Canadian majority culture when they were ready to participate in it fully. All the ethnic groups, therefore, were eager to break down this rigid vertical mosaic.

In Montreal, the first group of outsiders to gain full admittance to Anglo-Protestant society were the Jews. They first pressed the schools to open their doors to Jewish children, who until the 1930s were turned away by certain Anglo-Protestant school boards. Jewish children were finally accepted when the provincial government created a Jewish school board whose sole mandate was to negotiate a contract with the Anglo-Protestant boards for admission of Jewish students. It is interesting to note that at the time, leaders of French Catholic society pushed cultural pluralism on the Protestants, and through legislation imposed on the English community attitudes of tolerance which they themselves refused to practise.

Until World War II, McGill University also discriminated against Jewish students by insisting they attain higher entrance marks than other ethnic groups. During this same period, Anglo-Protestant hospitals such as the Royal Victoria and the Montreal General admitted only limited numbers of Jewish interns and rarely offered them top appointments. It was in response to these policies that the Jewish community raised funds to open the Jewish General Hospital of Montreal.

After World War II, the anglophone elites became more accepting of ethnic minorities. Nevertheless, until 1960, access to top positions in the English community was difficult. Jews and other immigrants could start different sorts of small businesses and act as professionals for their own communities, but they were not accepted by the inner circles of the big financial institutions, the school boards, or McGill University.

When this exclusivism finally ended, once again it was at the instigation of a provincial government which preferred to impose pluralism upon the English community rather than the French. In the early sixties, the Lesage government passed a law changing the constitution of the Protestant School Board of Greater Montreal to guarantee the Jewish minority five members. Around this time other barriers fell: the Montreal Stock Exchange began to admit Jewish brokers, McGill University finally accepted Samuel Bronfman on its board of governors, and several private clubs changed their admission regulations.

Having obtained access to the most important positions in the social and economic institutions of the English community, the leaders of the Jewish group decided to bury their memories of discrimination and identify with anglophone interests. This liaison intensified with the rise of nationalism in Quebec, which Jews feared more than the discrimination formerly practised by the English. What they found threatening was the xenophobia which they thought nationalism fuelled and the pressures in favour of a homogeneous as opposed to a pluralistic society.

After accepting the Jews, the English community started to open up to Italians, Greeks, Blacks, and other ethnic groups. The turning point came in 1968 with the St. Leonard school crisis which unleashed a struggle for clientele between English and French institutions. The economic and social importance of the immigrants suddenly came to light. To their great surprise, the English realized that about half the members of their community were not of British origin. At that point, they resolved to change elements of their institutions to satisfy immigrant expectations. The English school boards hired Greek,

Black, and Italian teachers and placed them in administrative posts; English social agencies sought out "ethnic" social workers and community organizers; and governments and corporate trusts began to fund special studies on ethnic communities. The transformation of anglophone society in Montreal was so rapid that by the time the Parti Québécois came to power, it had practically caught up with other large cities on the continent in its acceptance of pluralism and cultural diversity. The old ethnic pyramid dominated by Anglo-Protestants was finally crumbling.

Just at the point where ethnic groups felt they were making headway with the English, the French decided to force the immigrants to join their community. To their dismay, the ethnic groups saw that they would have to start over and retrace with the French the painful steps they had taken with the English: first social exclusion, then adaptation, and finally an acceptance which was often based upon opportunism and condescension. The overwhelming preoccupation of the provincial authorities with the behaviour of the ethnic groups did not augur well. The exclusivism and chauvinism which inspired much of French nationalist opinion made the immigrants worry about the future of the communities they had created for themselves in the inner city. Greeks, Portuguese, Italians, and others need their so-called ghettos to soften their entry into North America. Many come from peasant backgrounds and find urban society disorienting; without their communities, which remind them of home, they could not survive psychologically.

The French, however, have always misunderstood the function of these communities and are unaware of the various stages of immigrant acculturation characteristic of immigrant cities such as New York, Boston, or Montreal. For the French, the "little Italies" of the city are a threat to Quebec culture and should be discouraged at all costs. This idea is often expressed in the French community even by progressive people such as *Le Devoir* editorial writer Lise Bissonnette, who has suggested that the immigration ministry do more "to stop consolidation of menacing ghettos." This assimilationist viewpoint is also found among top officials of the social affairs and immigration ministries.

These attitudes show that the French milieu in Quebec knows little about the history and sociology of North American immigration and the complex configuration of inter-ethnic relations that has resulted from it. Over the years, French-speaking Quebecers had contact with newcomers in the work force and in commerce, but it was not until 1968 that the provincial government began to take an official interest in them. This was the first break with the old approach which consisted of pushing immigrants into the anglophone community in order to preserve the homogeneity of French culture.

Primarily because of developments in the United States, ethnic minorities are conscious of their rights and resolute in defending them. Until recently, the French community had little experience with ethnic groups entering their institutions and demanding services to reflect their needs and expectations. This has led to the mistaken impression that coercive education legislation accompanied by encouragement of folklore traditions will result in the rapid assimilation of ethnic groups in Montreal.

One important aspect of the problem, which official policy ignores, concerns the differences in mentality which have always separated ethnic communities from French-speaking Quebecers. The most salient of these touch upon questions of saving and social advancement. Immigrants and francophones have always worked together in factories where jobs are tough and pay is low. For immigrants, these sweatshops represent the first step up the social ladder which they are determined to climb for themselves and for their children. Often in a single generation, immigrants move from ditch-digging to professional and managerial occupations.[1] To realize their ambitions, immigrants often work excessively long days under conditions which Canadian-born people will not accept. In most immigrant families, everyone works and often two or three families share a single apartment. They make these sacrifices so they can accumulate enough capital to escape from their situation and achieve a better standard of living. The francophones who work with these immigrants, however, do not have the same drives and ambitions. In contrast to the newcomers, francophones tend to see themselves as permanent members of the working class.

Often immigrants live in the same neighbourhoods as the French working class. After several years of intense saving, they buy duplexes and triplexes and slowly become the landlords of their less ambitious neighbours. The immigrants will also use their capital to open small manufacturing or construction businesses. This pattern arouses animosity towards the newcomers, who begin to monopolize certain kinds of employment and seem to prosper with mysterious facility. In the past this situation was complicated by the monopolization of finance and big business in Quebec by English and U.S. interests. As the newcomers acquired English, they made contacts with anglophone financial interests and drove many French Quebecers from the small businesses which had been their traditional economic strongholds. This lies at the root of some of the French suspicion of Jews and their later animosity towards Italians.[2]

Most immigrant groups continue to engage in this cycle of overwork, savings, and investment. During their first years in Quebec they congregate in their own communities, where they feel most comfortable. As they realize their ambitions, they usually move into sectors of the city which better reflect their new social situation. In Montreal the immigrant passage is quite clear. Jews started near the foot of St. Lawrence Boulevard in the centre of the city and progressed north. As they became more affluent, they moved west along Van Horne Avenue and finally settled in Cote St. Luc and the Town of Mount Royal. Greeks are now where Jews were forty years ago and the Portuguese are not far behind. Newly arrived Italians settle in the north of Montreal around the Jean Talon market. As they improve their status, they move to St. Michel or St. Leonard.

The relations which exist between the French and the Italians, who are more integrated into the francophone milieu than any other minority, suggest some of the problems which could emerge between ethnic groups and the French community in the future. Unlike other ethnic groups, the Italians tend to mingle socially with francophones and to live in French-speaking neighbourhoods. The older generation of Italians, for example, is far more fluent in French than in English. Nevertheless, differences in mentality always prevailed and these explain in large measure the problem which created the St. Leonard school crisis.

Like most newcomers, the Italians show more entrepreneurial spirit than most of the French-speaking population. For immigrants with little education, starting up a small business is often the only way they can improve their social and economic situation. Many start with tiny operations and move on from there to become contractors, restaurateurs, and real estate owners. Over the long term, however, the Italians believe that the most important avenue to a better standard of living is a good education for their children. They associate economic success with the English language, and have always sent their children to English schools even though they lived in predominantly French neighbourhoods.

For a long time, this choice did not pose problems. After all, 10 to 15 per cent of French parents were doing the same thing. Little by little, though, the Italian community became more English-speaking. The movement accelerated as better-educated and more prosperous members began to acquire interesting jobs in the English business milieu.

The purpose of Bill 101 was to stop this tendency among Italians and all other immigrants once and for all. After ten years of resistance to French nationalism, newcomers cannot ignore the pressures favouring the French language. The ethnic groups' fear of being excluded, however, was strongly revived by the preface to Bill 1, which was the first draft of Bill 101. It defined Quebecers as francophones only and thereby excluded all language minorities. The militant approach of the francophones in affirming their rights is now being repeated by the ethnic groups in defence of theirs. The minorities are becoming intent upon promoting their interests and their conception of Quebec society. Already many groups have told the provincial authorities that they expect the French majority to make major accommodations in the educational system, in social and health services, and in the public service.

The tensions of the last ten years contributed enormously to the political coming of age of ethnic groups in Montreal. This is clear from these extracts from a letter which appeared in the *Montreal Star* and *Le Devoir* in the spring of 1979. Insurance broker Paul Pantazis, who was asked by the provincial Liberal party to organize an ethnic groups symposium, had this to say:

> In the past, we so-called "new-Canadians" and "néo-Québécois" have not taken an active part in the Quebec political scene. We were never encouraged to contribute to shaping the policies for which we were asked to vote. Traditionally, political parties in Quebec have treated ethnic groups as surrogate English or French voters, but have ignored us as groups with distinct

identities having problems, interests and political ideas of our own.

Times have certainly changed. All of a sudden, we are being inundated with conferences, symposiums, ministerial visits and government grants. It is not surprising that after years of neglect, Quebec's ethnic minorities feel distrustful of these overtures.

No doubt, it is probably true that in many cases, the new interest in ethnic groups is not completely altruistic. As the history of conflict between the English and French in this country comes to a head, the two "founding peoples" have been forced to realize that they are not alone, but that another political force exists....

It is now possible for Quebec's ethnic groups to exploit their new "strategic eminence." We are now in a position to demand the full equality that still eludes us as "new-Canadians" and "néo-Québécois."

This letter shows that new Quebecers have no intention of severing their links with the English community. Rather than choosing to identify entirely with either of the two groups, they will attempt to draw from the best of both. The ethnic minorities are now ready to make their peace with the French population, but they still remember St. Leonard, they have not forgotten accusations that they take jobs away from French Quebecers, and they are still smarting from their exclusion in the first draft of Bill 101. Their integration into the French community will, as a result, be slow and cautious.

The Growth of a New Type of English Leadership

A long list of urgent telephone messages awaits Abe Limonchik when he arrives home from his job as a chemist at Domtar. Radio-Canada wants to interview him for a program on the new urban politics; Montreal Citizens Movement councillor Michael Fainstat would like to review some points for a City Hall debate; then there is a Parti Québécois activist from the radical Centre-Sud region, the Conservative candidate for Westmount, an English business executive, some worried immigrant parents, and a number of others.

Limonchik, who wears a beret and baggy pants and is affectionately known as "Boumie" to his friends, is president of City Hall's major opposition party. Formed five years ago, the Montreal Citizens Movement, or the Rassemblement des Citoyens de Montréal as it is called in French, is the only Quebec political party where French and English work together without linguistic problems. Limonchik quietly makes his calls, moving effortlessly from English to French, offering information and advice.

Abe Limonchik grew up in the 1940s and 50s on the periphery of the Jewish ghetto described by Mordecai Richler in *Duddy Kravitz* and *St. Urbain's Horseman*. Like many of his friends, he went to English schools but worked in the east end, where he learned French. His wife is French from Trois-Rivières and he has always moved with ease among

Quebecers of all stripes. He is a friend of union leader Michel Chartrand and knew Parti Québécois ministers Jacques-Yvan Morin and Robert Burns in the days when they all belonged to the Quebec wing of the New Democratic Party. However, Limonchik has always worked for Domtar, and as a result he is well acquainted with the English milieu and the business leaders who have acted on behalf of the anglophone community.

This capacity to be active at the core of both language communities has made Abe Limonchik an important political personage. For anglophones, who have been cut off from constructive political activity since the election of the Parti Québécois, he plays an important, perhaps crucial role. Five years ago when the Liberals were in power and anglophones could still depend upon the English business establishment for leadership, Limonchik was known to only a small coterie of intellectuals and social activists. Today, as the peripatetic Montreal Citizens Movement president, he has more political clout than the president of Domtar. Abe Limonchik is becoming the prototype of a new type of anglophone leader.

In the past, accommodation between the two solitudes took place quietly, in the offices, corridors, and backrooms of French politicians and English industrialists. As the Quebec bureaucracy grew, and as the idea of separate domains lost credibility among the French, these private arrangements became less and less workable. With the election of the Parti Québécois in 1976, the last vestiges of the old entente vanished. The English could no longer depend on business for a voice in Quebec affairs. Almost overnight, social action and municipal politics became the only meeting place for the two communities. Anglophones had to venture out into the majority French community and participate as individuals in political parties, unions, the civil service, social movements, and other important Quebec institutions.

Although most Montrealers are unaware of it, more and more anglophones are doing this. All over the city, other Abe Limonchiks are at work. These individuals are rising above the English community's ethnocentrism and abandoning the corporate elite's tendency to remain segregated. By personal example, they are joining mainstream Quebec and introducing the English community to new forms of participation and influence.

At the moment, this new group of people falls into five principal clusters. The first consists of Montreal Citizens Movement activists recruited from community organizers, social workers, lawyers, doctors, and other professionals. The second is composed of people from similar backgrounds who have worked in the anti-poverty, ecology, and women's movements. Individuals in both these fields slowly broke out of the confines of the English community through participation in the movements of the 1960s that started in the United States. Eventually they established links with French people working on the same issues.

A third key group consists of union leaders in English Protestant education who have allied with the Centrale de l'enseignement du Québec (the French teachers' union) to increase their bargaining power with the Quebec government. A much less visible category includes anglophones who have simply chosen to work in French milieus. Rather than pursuing careers with McGill University or the Royal Bank of Canada, they are at the Université du Québec à Montréal or Surveyer Nenniger & Chênevert.

A fifth stream of people stand out not so much for their daily activities as for their political stance. These people congregate in two quite different organizations. One is Participation Quebec, which encourages anglophones to integrate into French Quebec, although it strongly supports English culture and opposes assimilation. Members are young professionals in law, education, and business. The second is the

Committee of Anglophones for Sovereignty-Association, commonly referred to as CASA. Various polls show that between 10 and 25 per cent of English-speaking people feel sovereignty-association may be the solution to present problems in Quebec and Canada although they would not necessarily vote for it. CASA groups the tiny minority who feel strongly enough about sovereignty-association to campaign for it. Most CASA members are active Parti Québécois members who think sovereignty is the fastest and surest road to socialism in Quebec. At the present time, CASA is regarded with suspicion by most English-speaking people and is not taken seriously by Parti Québécois members or francophones in general. Nevertheless, the group receives a hearing and is not simply dismissed.

The social origins of the people in these various movements are quite different from those of the traditional English elite. Many come from poor immigrant and Jewish families who squeezed out a living in St. Lawrence Boulevard factories and never felt accepted by Anglo-Protestants. Quebecers of British origin are also part of this rising new leadership but many have come more recently from the United States, Britain, or other provinces, and feel detached from historic English-French antagonisms.

Politically, these people tend to federalism, although most believe that the status quo for the French in Quebec and Canada must change. All feel that the province's language of work should be French, but they also believe that the English-speaking community deserves official minority status and defined rights. Most find certain aspects of Bill 101 contrary to civil liberties, and most are wary of nationalism. But the language issue is not an obsession, and Quebec independence is not a threat. If the French majority wanted to separate from Canada they would accept the verdict and stay.

The new group of potential leaders tends to be ideologically left of centre. This is easy to explain. At this point, only social democrats seem interested in the type of grass-roots political activity which results in a common meeting ground for English and French. The more conservative elements in the English community still expect political action to come from the top.

Interestingly enough, although these people support French collective rights, they are more individualist than collectivist in their personal behaviour. Essentially, they are pioneering people who strike out on their own and display little attachment for any collectivities. This is partly because so many of them never identified wholly with either of Quebec's dominant cultures. In many ways, these people are culturally marginal men and women who tend to seek original solutions to social and political problems. It is precisely this talent that makes them valuable not only to the English community in particular but also to Quebec as a whole.

The experience and activities of these anglophones who are providing the English community with the possibility of a new orientation and leadership date to the mid-1960s, when they first became involved in the anti-poverty, women's, and ecology movements. These activists now work in a wide variety of grass-roots groups, among them neighbourhood legal aid clinics, tenants' rights organizations, women's centres, anti-nuclear associations and consumer protection groups. Some of these services are funded directly through the Quebec social affairs and justice ministries; others rely on special grants and volunteer labour.

What is important about the anglophones in these groups is that they work in a way that does not set them apart from the French majority. Because they accept French as the main language of work and do not insist upon special status for English, language and ethnicity are not issues. One example of this is the Pointe St. Charles and Little Burgundy legal aid clinic, which was started in 1970 by English-speaking students. Today the staff is mainly French and serves a largely French low-income population, but bilingual English-speaking lawyers are active.

The clinic operates in two communities which encompass many people on various forms of social assistance. Lawyers offer individual services to people suffering from welfare problems, landlord-tenant disputes, and so on, but they also work on broad community issues such as demolition, cooperative housing development, slum landlords, and day care. Their aim is to reduce discrimination against poor people in the application of laws and to press for legislative changes favourable to them.

English-speaking social activists working in organizations such as the Pointe St. Charles and Little Burgundy legal aid clinic are in some respects the most dynamic element of the rising new English leadership. However, they did not easily win their positions in the French majority community. Many underwent a painful apprenticeship when various English-based movements decided to work closely with their French counterparts. From this experience, these anglophones learned French and became more sensitive to the concerns of the majority. With the knowledge they acquired of French society, they moved into the centre of the French progressive movement and combined to form the Montreal Citizens Movement.

These English-speaking reformers differ from those who formed the backbone of the old CCF and NDP in Montreal. Instead of supporting an increase in federal government powers to reorganize society, they prefer a more decentralized government. This is a vital question in Quebec politics because of the desire of the French majority for more autonomy than is possible under the present constitution. These

English reformers, therefore, accept the general French political view and concentrate on local problems and issues directly related to individuals and smaller groups and communities.

As the NDP has been finding out in federal election campaigns, it is futile in Quebec to propose a strong central government as a means of achieving social justice and progress. It strikes no response at all among the French. Accordingly, English-speaking progressives in Montreal have given up on that kind of view, current among their counterparts in other provinces, and are working on different solutions.

In the late sixties when the new reformers began operating, their main concern was English welfare recipients in Pointe St. Charles and overworked immigrants in St. Louis and Park Extension. The favoured area for most of the reformers was "the Point," which has always been strongly Irish. There were clear reasons for this choice. French activists had a number of arenas to choose from: there were many French low-income neighbourhoods ripe for community work, a left-wing union movement, and of course nationalist political parties. English activists were more restricted, mainly because the Montreal English community has proportionately fewer poor people and a relatively small blue-collar labour force.

The 1960s were the time of the American war on poverty and the rise of neighourhood-power movements, and the theories of community organizer Saul Alinsky served as the inspiration for a new breed of social reformers. English-speaking social workers coming out of McGill University were influenced by these developments in the United States and they wanted a live community to work in. At the time, most did not speak French and knew little about French neighbourhoods. As a result, they flocked to "the Point," which had the largest concentration of English-speaking poor in the city. Working from this tiny base, they started an anti-poverty movement on the American model, and gained important social reforms in Quebec.

The key organizer of the movement was Peter Katadotis, a McGill School of Social Work graduate familiar with groups in the underbelly of the city. As a youth Katadotis washed dishes in his father's restaurant; later he worked in construction to save money for university. Fluent in English, French, and Greek, Katadotis moved in three cultural worlds, but because of his English education his base of operations was English.

Armed with a grant of a quarter of a million dollars from the McConnell Foundation, Katadotis in 1969 set up the Parallel Institute in the basement of a United Church mission house in Pointe St. Charles. The aim of the movement was power to poor people and the organizing model came from Saul Alinsky. Since there were so many welfare recipients in Pointe St. Charles, the first target seemed obvious: improvement of welfare legislation.

Largely as a result of Katadotis' Pointe St. Charles team, the Greater Montreal Anti-Poverty Coordinating Committee, composed of seventeen mostly-English anti-poverty citizens' committees from the city's poor neighbourhoods, mounted a two-year welfare-rights campaign against the Quebec government. Welfare cheques rose, invasion of privacy was reduced, and more generous welfare regulations were implemented.

Although most of the city's welfare recipients were French, the push for change came mainly from anglophone organizers and poor people. Later a network of francophone welfare action groups was set up by French organizers, but at the time most of the French reformers thought the welfare-rights issue did not figure in the grand scheme of social change. CSN leader Michel Chartrand, for example, initially refused even moral support to groups because he felt their aims conflicted with his revolutionary interests.

The launching of the most avant-garde legal aid system in the country was also largely attributable to English activists in Pointe St. Charles. The germ began with some McGill law students who in 1970 set up a community legal aid clinic of the American storefront type. The main goal of the clinic was to develop a poor people's approach to the law on tenant questions, bailiff seizures, urban renewal, and so on. The first employee was McGill University law graduate Robert Cooper, who came to the attention of Liberal Justice Minister Jérôme Choquette. The minister asked Cooper to become a special adviser on new legal aid legislation and the result was Bill 10, which provides three types of legal aid: community-controlled clinics, government-run legal aid centres, and a system where individual lawyers can be chosen by the client and paid for by the government.

Quebec's legal aid legislation is considered more appropriate for low-income people than the Ontario plan. Unfortunately neither the Liberal nor the Parti Québécois government has encouraged establishment of the community-controlled clinics. They have feared that the clinics will be taken over by Marxist-Leninist activists, who wreaked havoc in many organizations in the mid-1970s.

Of the three community-controlled services that exist, two were started by anglophones and still have English-speaking staff, although most of the work and clientele is now French. One is the Pointe St. Charles clinic; the other is Services Juridiques St-Louis on St. Hubert Street, which was started by lawyer Zyskind Finkelstein when he was still a student at McGill University. Although the government dropped the clinic from official legal aid funding two years ago, Finkelstein and three other lawyers are keeping the service financially afloat and responsive to community issues.

Another area where anglophone reformers made an important contribution was in non-profit cooperative housing for poor people. This type of housing started in 1973 when the federal government's Central Mortgage and Housing Corporation began providing special low-interest mortgages for non-profit projects under a National Housing Act amendment. Cooperative housing, however, began to proliferate only in 1977 when the new Parti Québécois government provided funding for special cooperative-housing consultant organizations.

Well before the housing act amendment, however, anglophone architects, town planners, and students associated with the Parallel Institute founded an important low-income cooperative housing scheme which served as a training ground for later projects. Loge Peuple de Pointe St. Charles was the name of the experiment, which in 1970 received $1 million in mortgage money from the CMHC to rehabilitate 100 housing units for poor people. The project coordinators were McGill architect Joseph Baker, who later became director of Laval University's school of architecture, and City of Montreal town planner Andy Melamed, who now teaches at Concordia University's new School of Community and Public Affairs.

From the project came expertise which contributed significantly to the growth of cooperative housing for the city's low-income people. Two important people in this regard were Ernest Vaudry, a Pointe St. Charles resident who became a Loge Peuple tenant, and James McGregor, who studied town planning at the Université de Montréal. Together they set up the Conseil de Développement du Logement Communautaire, which is now the most effective consulting group in the field. Although the organization is mostly French, its leaders are anglophones who started in Pointe St. Charles with the English anti-poverty movement.

During the late sixties and early seventies the French reformers adopted a different style and orientation from that of the English. Swept up in the tide of nationalism, the French tended to want broad political and social changes for the whole of Quebec society, while the English who were influenced by the Americans tended to stress reform. In this context, the fledgling Parti Québécois was extremely important for many French activists. So was the union movement, which pushed for health and security reforms in factories, construction sites, and mines, and mounted a massive campaign to save low-income consumers from exploitation by finance companies.

Unionism and provincial politics were closed to the English because of the isolation of the community from the French majority and the small numbers of English-speaking people in unionized jobs. The "national question" was also difficult terrain. Because of these restrictions, English activists developed community organizing among a small group of welfare poor into a fine art, and in a short time secured lasting reforms for a broad band of poor Quebecers.

French activists were also involved in the neighbourhood power movement, but because of nationalist feeling they were hesitant to work with the English. Shortly after his arrival in Pointe St. Charles, Peter Katadotis tried to organize a Conseil de Quartier for all organizers and citizens' groups in the area but the plan failed, largely because the French feared the English would dominate. In 1972, during a strong nationalist wave among many activist groups, the French staff of the Parallel Institute resigned, and thus accentuated the cultural and linguistic division between English and French progressives. The English continued their work, although the split caused a painful reassessment of their approach and activities. Slowly they started to function more in French. Eventually the organizations they started became mostly French and they themselves blended into the French mainstream community where many of them are today.

A similar sort of integration took place in the women's movement, which also experienced a cultural and linguistic crisis in 1972. Although they are now more conservative, English feminists played an important role in lighting the first women's liberation fires in Quebec, mainly because of the influence of American feminists. The movement gained impetus in 1968 when McGill student activists Donna Cherniak and Allan Feingold produced a revolutionary but highly informative birth-control handbook. This book, which became an immediate best-seller, has sold over ten million copies in English and French in Canada and the United States. To handle the soaring demand for the book from women's groups and colleges, a non-profit publishing house called Montreal Health Press was eventually set up. It continues to publish feminist-oriented books in English and French on various subjects.

Birth control and then abortion soon became central feminist issues for both French and English women. At the beginning English and French feminists met together, but quickly parted and formed the Front de libération des femmes and Montreal Women's Liberation. Although the organizations were separate, they joined to do abortion counselling. At the time only the French were bilingual, so they agreed to do abortion counselling for both language groups. In 1972, however, the French decided they would no longer offer abortion counselling in English.

This angered the English feminists who were suddenly forced to set up their own abortion counselling centre. The conflict nevertheless encouraged English feminists to push beyond feminist issues to examine the changes taking place in Quebec society at large. After that English feminists slowly learned French and joined the French feminist network, although they still serve mostly English-speaking women.

English and French feminists have perceived women's liberation in different terms. The French see the movement as part of a vast program of social reform which includes Quebec independence. As a result they have tended to press for collective solutions in questions of employment, child care, and marriage law. The English have stressed the individual and therefore tended to emphasize personal counselling on such questions as abortion, divorce, and back-to-work problems.

The ecology movement was much slower to gain a French character because the French became interested in environmental issues much later. Save Montreal, STOP, Green Spaces, the James Bay Committee, and the Canadian Coalition for Nuclear Responsibility, for example, were all largely English-speaking. One of the first ecology organizations to shift from English to French was Citizens on Cycles, now Le Monde à Bicyclette. Its founder, Bob Silverman, pushed the bicycle movement into the French community because he realized the lobby needed a French political base to secure bicycle paths and changes in traffic regulations. Another organization which began in English and later penetrated the French community is the Automobile Protection Association run by consumer advocate Phil Edmonston. Edmonston, who is known as Phil in English and Louis-Philippe in French, has written over a dozen books on the consumer and the car, and has carved out a name for himself as the Ralph Nader of Quebec.

About 1973, the effectiveness of extra-parliamentary activity was fading and many English-speaking social activists in the anti-poverty, women's, and ecology movements began to look for other fields of action. With their knowledge of French and their awareness of Montreal social problems, many felt ready to move into the political arena. Provincial politics seemed difficult because of the independence issue. Consequently, they turned to city politics where language, sovereignty-association, and other controversial problems could be more easily ignored.

At the municipal level, they could combine with the French on the basis of a common vision of what Montreal should be: a city with decision-making from the neighbourhoods up, implementing ideas of ecological balance and amenity. With this goal, English and French progressive forces in citizens' groups, the Parti Québécois, the NDP, and the unions were able to coalesce in a way never before possible. The result was the Montreal Citizens Movement, founded in 1974. In the municipal election held that year, the MCM won 45 per cent of the popular vote and eighteen out of fifty-four council seats. Almost overnight, the party was an important political force in the city.

It is important to note that this coalition took place during a period of mounting social tension between English and French over language issues. Language never became a point of contention in the MCM. When divisions in the movement surfaced, they were over ideological questions. Acceptance of French as the language of the central office and the party as a whole helped the spirit of cooperation between English and French. Each riding, however, operated in the language of the majority of its members. At general party congresses representatives were encouraged to speak in either English or French, and everyone was expected to understand.

As the movement stepped up its activities after the election, the English assumed a high profile in the party. The English middle-class neighbourhood of Notre Dame de Grace became the party's model of participation and organization. City councillor Michael Fainstat succeeded in creating an alliance of widely differing groups, among them tenants, senior citizens, environmentalists, members of the professions, and small businessmen.

Barely a year after the 1974 election, English leftists provoked irreconcilable divisions in the new party. They placed ideological discussion before social action and dragged the party into interminable debates which cut the party off from its grass-roots support and alienated activists eager to tackle practical community issues. Leftists such as Stephen Schecter, Henry Milner, and councillor John Gardiner created such dissension that the MCM could not effectively fight the 1978 municipal election.

The more conservative wing of the party led by councillors Nick Auf der Maur and Bob Keaton also weakened the movement. Both were forced to leave the party when they ran in the 1976 provincial elections. When they sought readmission after their defeat, the left rallied enough votes to keep them out. The pair, however, was already impatient with the MCM policy that political action should flow from neighbourhood organizations and groups. Both believed that the caucus of elected councillors should guide their attitudes and decisions. Auf der Maur and Keaton, although social democrats, belonged to a more traditional school of media politicians who rely more upon impressing the press and large groups than cultivating close contacts with constituents. Angered by the obstruction of the left, the two decided to participate in founding the rival Municipal Action Group under Serge Joyal. The result was to be expected: the opposition was split and both groups were routed by Jean Drapeau. The only two opposition members elected were Michael Fainstat and Nick Auf der Maur.

After the election, the Municipal Action Group disintegrated and the MCM began rebuilding its membership and its image. Despite its reduced impact on the city, the Montreal Citizens Movement continues to be an important instrument of integration into Quebec society for anglophones. Through this municipal party they are entering majority politics and paving the way toward participation at the provincial level once the "national question" is more settled.

The union movement has also served as an important vehicle for integration of anglophones into the new politics of Quebec. Very early on it became clear to union leaders of English schoolteachers, community college professors, and nurses that they must join their French counterparts. With the government takeover of education and social and health services, employer-union relations took a new form. The Quebec bureaucracy wanted uniformity in contracts and this required union coordination in the public and parapublic sectors.

The Provincial Association of Protestant Teachers (PAPT), which represents about 6,500 teachers across the province, is one of the best union examples of English willingness to participate in Quebec life. The PAPT is particularly interesting because of its decision in 1967 to ally itself with the French teachers' union, the Corporation des enseignants du Québec (later called the Centrale de l'enseignement du Québec), though nothing compelled it to do so at the time. For several more years, the association could have continued signing friendly agreements with the Protestant school boards.

In 1967 the government passed a law establishing province-wide collective bargaining for teachers. The PAPT, however, was still not a union and its affiliates had never negotiated contracts. Because of this, the government said that if the PAPT did not seek union status, the Protestants could sidestep the bill. Eager to avoid provincial negotiations and to keep as much autonomy as possible, the Protestant School Board of Greater Montreal offered the Montreal Teachers Association a good contract, which the government promised to extend to all PAPT members. But the PAPT chose unionism and provincial negotiations in preference to friendly deals with the school boards.

The importance of this decision cannot be exaggerated. In a way, the PAPT broke Anglo-Protestant solidarity toward French society. It recognized that the historical isolation of the two societies could no longer endure. This showed clarity of vision that few English institutions exhibited at the time. To have their say in education, the Protestant teachers realized that they had to ally with the French majority in the CEQ.

This dramatic gesture was not made without creating serious problems. The only bilingual union leader was Donald Peacock, president of the MTA and vice-president of the PAPT, a native of the United Kingdom and a socialist activist. Without him, the Protestant teachers organization would surely have collapsed. At the time, the English rank-and-file teachers tended to a conservative outlook and saw themselves as professionals, not unionists; the prospect of strikes and picket lines was distasteful. In addition, they found the idea of associating with the nationalist CEQ unnerving.

Despite all these reservations, the PAPT and the CEQ succeeded in jointly negotiating four collective agreements after 1967. Eventually, the law was amended to permit separate negotiations, which the PAPT refused. The only union to adopt this option was the Provincial Association of Catholic Teachers. Anglo-Catholic education is administratively part of the French system, and the union preferred to keep its distance.

The collaboration between the Protestant teachers and the CEQ was maintained throughout the whole period of linguistic tension, notably during the St. Leonard riots when francophone teachers demanded more severe laws to prevent integration of immigrants into anglophone schools. The anglophone union leaders overcame these community and political antagonisms and acquired a better knowledge of the

French milieu, which helped them avoid certain painful errors.

Inspired by healthy realism, the PAPT refused to accept the infringements on the collective agreement that inevitably would have been produced by the clandestine admission into the Protestant school system of children excluded by Bill 101 in 1977. The union considered that this gesture would only have led to a sterile confrontation with the French majority. Much more realistic than school administrators, these unions prepared the way for better understanding between the two main linguistic communities of Quebec.

Personal integration into French society obviously takes place through groups and institutions. The anglophones active in citizens' groups, in the Montreal Citizens Movement, and in unions had to adapt to French society to avoid marginalization of the groups whose interests they were defending. Nevertheless, there are many anglophones who are responding to the present situation as individuals. They have alternatives not open to groups and institutions: they can remain at home in segregated English communities or they can emigrate to other regions of Canada where the linguistic complications of Montreal do not exist.

Another possibility is to venture into the majority French society. The avenue most often chosen is the workplace. Instead of pursuing a career in English institutions like the federal civil service or the Sun Life Assurance Company, some people have turned to the Université de Montréal, to public companies like Sidbec and Hydro-Quebec, or to the Montreal municipal administration. A significant number of people have chosen to move out of their element even though they have only a rudimentary knowledge of French and vague notions of what French society is all about.

French-language universities have a significant number of anglophones on their teaching staffs. Some examples at the Université de Montréal are American linguist Kathleen Connors, Ontario economist Leonard Dudley, and psychologist Ethel Roskies, who is of Montreal Jewish background. Roskies' views are typical of many Jews and immigrants who started off in the English community and then moved to the French one. "We always felt marginal to the English community, which wasn't that welcoming to Jews. Since we knew we would always be marginal, it didn't really matter which community we were marginal in. In some sense we would always be outsiders."

The provincial and municipal civil services also have some anglophones, of whom an example is architect Alex Kowaluk. He works for the City of Montreal's planning department. Like Roskies, he never felt strongly attached to the English community. Born in Montreal of Ukrainian working-class parents, he went to McGill University and worked for various English architectural firms for several years. Although he spoke no French, he nevertheless decided to take the plunge into the French work milieu: "I wasn't really interested in private enterprise. In addition, I didn't feel accepted by the English because of my background. I liked the French and wanted to participate in Quebec life."

During this time of political tension, it would appear that few anglophone businessmen would leave English jobs for French ones. Yet the number of English-speaking people in French business establishments is growing. The Caisses Populaires Desjardins credit union movement, engineering consulting firms such as Surveyer Nenniger & Chênevert, Hydro-Quebec, and Sidbec all have anglophones who work in French with few problems.

Terence Dancy, a Sidbec executive, was born in Great Britain and worked in the American steel industry until he was recruited by Sidbec. He arrived in 1970 at the height of the October Crisis but took the political situation in stride. Although he knew no French upon arrival, he immersed himself in the language and is now fluent. Businessmen and professionals working in French companies keep a low political profile and carefully avoid controversy, but their personal experience has an impact on the English community by helping to break down old barriers.

The most controversial group of anglophones playing new roles in Quebec consists of those who support sovereignty-association. Lawyer Paul Unterberg was the first anglophone to run for the Parti Québécois in a provincial election. The second was David Levine, an adviser to Economic Development Minister Bernard Landry who ran against Liberal Herbert Marx in the D'Arcy McGee byelection of 1979.

There are two anglophone civil servants on the political staff of the party in power. They are David Payne, a British immigrant and former Montreal CEGEP teacher who is now an adviser to Cultural Development Minister Camille Laurin, and David Levine, who directed a local community service centre until he joined Landry. Apart from these three, about 200 anglophone members of the Parti Québécois are active in several ridings.

In addition to the anglophone "Péquistes," two English-speaking pressure groups which support sovereignty-association but not necessarily the Parti Québécois have also emerged. One was called Comité anglophone pour un Québec unifié. This was a loose association of young English-speaking leftists who supported certain aspects of Bill 101 and in a brief to the National Assembly dissociated itself from the views of the English economic elite. The group has since disbanded.

The other group is the Committee of Anglophones for Sovereignty-Association (CASA), which was created specifically to campaign in favour of sovereignty-association. Its president is Henry Milner, an activist on the left wing of the Montreal Citizens

Movement, a college teacher, and author of two books on Quebec. Among other members are Robert Dean, regional director of the United Auto Workers union; sociologist Gary Caldwell; and Donald Waye, an engineer with Surveyer Nenniger & Chênevert.

The purpose of CASA is twofold. It first wants to persuade anglophones of the merits of political sovereignty for Quebec coupled with economic association with the rest of Canada. Secondly, it wants to make the French population aware of the varied composition of the English community in Quebec. According to CASA, sovereignty-association is a political option which should not be coloured by language or ethnicity. In its view, a situation where all independentists are French and all English are federalists is dangerous and should be discouraged.

At this point, anglophones who actively support sovereignty and work in CASA are considered a strange and traitorous breed by a good part of the English community. Even among most of the French, who associate sovereignty with nationalist feelings, they are looked upon with suspicion. Eventually, political choices may be dictated not by nationalism and cultural identity but by a desire to break through the constitutional impasse in Canada. Most Quebec anglophones, however, feel strongly attached to Canada as a historical entity and cannot countenance a break in the political unity of the country.

It is from these different milieus, which are at the moment marginal, that the potential for a different type of English community and a new style of leadership is growing. The rigid approach of the present economic elite, their incapacity to understand cultures and aspirations different from their own, and their tendency to leave Quebec make certain changes inevitable.

The people who are exploring new types of relations with the French milieu are not numerous. However, they will soon be joined by young people from French immersion programs and French schools. Although many are not completely fluent in French, they are growing up with different views on Quebec. What is important about these individuals is not their political orientation but their intellectual curiosity, flexibility, and capacity to accept change.

As a result of the political and economic changes in Quebec, these people are questioning the traditional hierarchy of the English community and the role of business; they are asserting new values in an effort to build a society more sensitive to social as opposed to purely economic goals. This reassessment is affecting the English community at large, which more and more is abandoning its dependence on business and venturing into new cultural and educational fields.

The end of English control over the economy and the rise of a new English bilingualism and biculturalism will radically alter the political behaviour of the English community. This shift will boost the community's social and economic credibility, which is now lower than ever.

The English community is not yet aware of the transformation it is undergoing. One of the reasons for this is the incapacity of the anglophone media to deal with any question that contradicts the conventional wisdom on the community's social needs and policies. Very little time and space are given to movements that are foreshadowing the change.

One group which benefits from media attention is the Positive Action Committee, formed after the 1976 election to fight for English language rights and against sovereignty-association. However, the absence of any social critique from the movement shows clearly that it is not interested in promoting fundamental changes in English-French relations and that its main interest is defence of the status quo.

The career of Reed Scowen in the Quebec Liberal party illustrates the difficulties of healthy public discussion. Scowen, who started in business and later became a federal civil servant, was elected for the first time to the National Assembly in a 1978 byelection in Notre Dame de Grace in Montreal. A native of the Eastern Townships, he is trying to rally the English community to a more realistic view of its situation in Quebec.

According to Scowen, the nature of Canadian federalism dictates that the fate of the English community be in the hands of the French majority, which in its own interests cannot allow itself to be too rigid. This situation leaves room for negotiation on two principal points: recognition of the predominance of French on one hand, and of English minority rights on the other. The cold reception these ideas have received in the media and in public opinion indicates that the anglophone population is still a long way from this kind of hypothesis and that it still tends to rely on the federal power and on Canadian economic institutions to re-establish its position.

The new aspect of Scowen's strategy resides in the view that the English community still possesses bargaining power independent of its economic base and can use it to defend its collective interests. This power, which Scowen wants to use at the provincial level through the Liberal party, rests in effect on the penetration of the new anglophone elite into the French milieu through its various community activities.

The New Canadian Economic Society

The clash between English and French in Quebec, and its repercussions on the workings of the federal system, are among the most critical problems facing the country. Some believe the issue can be resolved by new constitutional arrangements and a new economic deal for the French. The most pessimistic scenarios anticipate that Canada will break up and Quebec will sink into chaos. There are also fears that Montreal's English community will be driven out of the province by a vengeful government eager to do away with the last vestiges of the Battle of the Plains of Abraham.

Nevertheless, the present conflict is much broader in scope than a competition between French and English for power in politics and business. It is really an upheaval in the basic organization of Canadian society.

French nationalism in Quebec, which is seen as the source of present tensions, is in reality only one facet of the profound transformation which has affected all of Canada. If Quebec has been marked by the economic decline of Montreal, so has the rest of the country. The social and economic structures associated with what has been called the Commercial Empire of the St. Lawrence could not survive very long after the eclipse of its historical base.

French discontent, as expressed since 1960, is concerned with casting off the historical roles or domains that had been attributed and accepted as British rule settled on Quebec after 1759. This ethnic division of labour allowed the English full control over the economy while the French had to be content with the sphere of culture and social organization. It was on this basis that the French later adjusted to the ethnic pyramid which appeared in Canada with the first waves of non-British and non-Protestant immigrants in the nineteenth century. But it has remained an incomplete adaptation because French Quebec could never make a permanent and clear-cut decision whether it should identify with the Canadian economy or retain its historical marginality.

The French never had any direct experience of immigration, except that it helped to confirm their minority status and introduced new competitors in commercial and cheap-labour occupations. But immigration has played a key role in the development of English Canada, and today its contribution is more important than ever.

The first waves of non-British immigrants went westwards. Ukrainians and Germans set up agricultural communities where their cultural values and even their language could survive. Immigrants also banded together in the cities, where ethnic ghettos met most of their social needs. The latest arrivals, usually destitute and uneducated, started at the bottom of the social ladder. Because of their willingness to work long hours at low pay, and their high propensity to save, they soon managed to improve their condition. They integrated into the mainstream of Canadian life while preserving their language and culture for two or three generations. Yet as individuals and as groups, they recognized the existence of an ethnic pyramid at the top of which were the Anglo-Protestants, closely identified with management of the economy. It took a very long time for this social model to be challenged. It seemed a natural state of affairs, in spite of the crippling disadvantages which might result for individuals and groups.

In addition to their tendency to congregate in urban ghettos, ethnic groups also tended to be concentrated in certain occupations, such as Jews in the needle trades, Italians in the construction industry, Chinese in laundry and restaurant services, Blacks in hotels and railway services, and so on. This pattern of occupational ghettos, which closely resembled that in the United States, created links between ethnicity and occupation and between ethnicity and social class.

It was not until the 1960s that this kind of ethnic stratification was perceived as inherently wrong and oppressive. As late as 1957, Prime Minister Louis Saint-Laurent campaigned on a promise to strengthen what he usually called "the Canadian Mosaic." His aim was to promote greater acceptance of ethnic diversity and a better understanding of the cultural contribution made by immigrants and French Canadians. But there was nothing to indicate that the Liberal party intended to level the ethnic pyramid and to bring changes to the exercise of economic power in the country. The expression used by Saint-Laurent was ironically echoed some eight years later in the title of a book by Canadian sociologist John Porter, *The Vertical Mosaic*. It described the nature and extent of Anglo-Protestant power over Canada's ethnic pyramid.

Ethnic stratification in Canada gave way before becoming a serious social issue. Numerous factors contributed to the abandonment of the so-called mosaic, but the most important one might well have been the growing industrial demand for a better educated and more sophisticated labour force. Mass education, with its availability to a wider range of classes and groups in society, made it more difficult to maintain the discriminatory practices of the past. Members of ethnic groups, who had been confined to

certain categories of low-paying jobs, developed greater expectations and could enjoy broader professional
horizons, even if racist or ethnic animosities still
prevail among the majority.

Simultaneously, bureaucratic trends in government and in private enterprise brought about new job
specifications which reduced most clerical and blue-
collar tasks to a series of simple and repetitive
gestures. While in the past certain jobs leading to
social advancement may have required some of those
mysterious qualifications that only dominant groups
seem to possess, the new ones with their simplified
contents were accessible to the graduates which a
reformed educational system was turning out by the
thousands. It was about the same time, between 1950
and 1960, that industry in Canada began making
serious use of objective criteria for the hiring and
promotion of staff. Although application of the various
merit systems retained certain biases, against Blacks
and women for instance, they still helped to avert the
build-up of ethnic tensions that a stratified society
would have inevitably experienced.

The ethnic pyramid survived longer in Montreal,
where Anglo-Protestant elements continued to exercise a local influence that no longer bore any relation
to their power over the Canadian economy. The
pluralism that was changing the rest of the country
took longer to affect Montreal. One possible explanation may be that the city's economic life has been
dominated by banks and various financial institutions
that happen to be unusually conservative in their
social outlook. Furthermore, not only had Montreal
lost its leadership, but it had become increasingly
isolated from the Canadian mainstream.

If Montreal failed to move with the rest of the
country it was that the French were not really
interested in the pluralism that was fast becoming the
rule in the English-speaking provinces. As a group,
the French were not eager to join the Canadian

mainstream except on their own terms: acceptance of their language and of their culture by the public service and the corporate establishment of Canada. The basic drive of French nationalism has not been to obtain equality of opportunity for individuals. Its main objective was to gain a share of the historical power wielded by the Anglo-Protestants.

Unfortunately, after World War II, this power was no longer there to be shared. It was rapidly draining away towards Toronto and the West, and Quebec nationalism accelerated the corporate exodus. At the same time this threatening nationalism helped to perpetuate acceptance of English leadership among the city's various ethnic groups, who had no understanding at all of the historical subtleties behind the claims and the animosity of the nationalists.

The persistence of ethnic stratification in Montreal shows in a variety of ways. The question of ethnic ties occupies a disproportionate amount of time in political discourses, which in most cases attempt to cater to them. The defensive and conservative attitudes adopted everywhere on this question are ultimately reflected in the economy. It is difficult to establish how much ethnic identification has contributed to the somewhat stagnant climate of Montreal, but it certainly has helped to perpetuate outmoded procedures and institutions and hindered the emergence of a more creative and stimulating relationship between the various elements in the city. Only a pluralistic society, where discrimination and exclusiveness are no longer institutionalized, would allow Quebec to recover a more optimistic view of politics. As it is, Montreal finds it difficult to go beyond the traditional "Canadian Mosaic."

It was inevitable that some of the cultural and ethnic tensions of Canada should find expression in territorial claims. In this respect, there is a certain analogy between the attitudes of the French in Quebec and those of the Indians in the Northwest

Territories collectively known as the Déné nation. The economic exclusion practised by the dominant English-speaking group has induced both the French and the Dénés to fall back on their own culture and to seek its establishment on a given territory which might be considered exclusively their own. The control of natural resources demanded by the Dénés is actually a line of defence to protect their environment and their mode of life against the ravages of excessive development characteristic of the white man's economy. This demand has been rejected by the federal government on the grounds that under these circumstances a Déné state or province would necessarily be racist. This is the same argument invoked against an independent Quebec, which could be expected to abrogate most of the cultural and linguistic rights of the English community there, not to mention its economic power.

The business leaders of English Canada have always been adamant about not giving up their control of the economy, not only when other groups have demanded their share of power but also when challenged on a territorial basis. It was this attitude which was behind the attempts of 1840 to destroy the political base of the French, the decision to crush the Métis Rebellion in Saskatchewan in 1885, and the refusal to countenance Indian claims that might hinder the dominant type of economic development. It is the same attitude which prevents the federal government from entertaining any notion of negotiating with the Parti Québécois on independence or even sovereignty-association.

Yet, just as in the case of the ethnic pyramid, there are indications of impending changes in the way territorial integrity or completeness is conceived. Not surprisingly, the most important sign of change comes from Quebec. Faced with demands on the part of the French middle class for greater participation in the management of the Canadian economy, many large national corporations seem ready to allow, as an alternative to power-sharing, the creation of a French business preserve within Quebec. There is a willingness to abandon the direct control which has been historically maintained over the Quebec economy and to give up the management of local branches and subsidiaries to the increasingly aggressive new class of French managers who can be expected to gradually assert their independence from head offices and shareholders outside the province. The exodus of head-office functions foreshadows the growing independence of this new class of French managers just as it announces the balkanization of the unitary economy which had always been controlled by a single ethnic group.

The management of the country's economic activity is currently undergoing significant changes. It is generally assumed that the exodus of corporate head offices from Montreal results in a single new decision centre in Toronto. However, this migration is not reproducing the concentration of power that was characteristic of Montreal in its heyday. While Toronto is attracting a growing number of head offices and is becoming a centre of financial services, managerial functions tend increasingly to be dispersed across the country as the regional sentiments which centralization once suppressed begin to express themselves more aggressively.

For the last 100 years or so, ever since the Prairies were opened to settlement, Canadian prosperity has been based on a form of regional specialization which encouraged the most efficient production of manufactured goods, agricultural staples, and raw materials. This was a vital necessity for a sparsely settled country whose export trade represented a substantial proportion of its income. Government policy, particularly with respect to freight rates and development grants, was designed to make exports more competitive in foreign markets. It was also designed to increase Canada's productive capacities in wheat, lumber, metals, fisheries, and selected types of manufacturing. The freight rates enforced in different parts of the country not only encouraged regional specialization but actually discouraged more diversified economic pursuits. Regions were prisoners of the economic roles assigned to them.

The fact that Canada was primarily a promoter's and a middleman's economy made it possible for much of the proceeds of production to be channelled towards financial institutions as speculative profits. These were usually re-invested in large-scale projects, often supported by public funds, which perpetuated the kind of lopsided development that had long been characteristic of Canada. The effects of the regional division of labour in the Canadian economy, of regional specialization, were felt in other negative ways. One major disadvantage was that it left the population of vast areas virtually at the mercy of the ups and downs of the business cycle and with few alternative sources of employment and income.

In the early part of the twentieth century, popular movements began to attack this state of affairs. They included populists and progressives, along with various farmers' coalitions. Later there were parties of the right such as Social Credit and parties of the left such as the Co-operative Commonwealth Federation, which subsequently transformed itself into the New Democratic Party in the idealistic expectation of an effective alliance between farmers and labour. In Quebec during the 1930s, the Action Libérale Nationale engaged in a vigorous battle against what it called the electricity trust and against financial operators who were causing the costs of various public services to rise outrageously.

All these movements, with their contradictory and competing ideologies, were in basic agreement on one fundamental objective: to throw off the control which financial institutions exerted over government, local business, agriculture, and people themselves. This kind of reform would favour the development of a more diversified regional economy, one that could offer better protection against monopolies and cartels, and against ruinous fluctuations in agricultural prices and in the level of industrial employment.

Political action held out the promise of legislation to improve the bargaining power of individual producers against that of the powerful coalition of speculators, international buyers, and bankers in various commodities produced for export. Some improvements did occur in response to political pressure as governments intervened to bring about more balanced marketing conditions. Similarly, social legislation helped cushion the harshest blows of the business cycle, as did cooperatives and government-supported lending institutions which helped protect the investments of individual farmers.

New forms of discontent began to appear with improvements in economic security, and they bore a striking resemblance to those that had challenged the ethnic pyramid. In one case as in the other the very narrow range of personal and group opportunities became unbearable. Mass education, which has undermined the ethnic division of labour in large Canadian cities, has similarly worked to end the regional division of labour in the Canadian economy. Local populations began to resent the social and economic limits imposed upon them, and they refused to content themselves with the vocations which national policies assigned to them and to their region. They insisted on greater occupational diversity without having to emigrate to other parts of the country.

Quebec was particularly sensitive to this issue since it suffered from both the ethnic and the regional division of labour, one handicap serving to reinforce the other. With the advent of the Quiet Revolution in 1960, the government made a serious attempt to diversify the province's economic base. It nationalized private power companies to obtain some leverage on development, and it laid the groundwork for an integrated steel industry. It moved to free itself from the influence of the banks and other lending institutions by setting up the Quebec Pension Plan, which could operate in a way comparable to that of a central bank and whose accumulated funds could be administered in accordance with provincial priorities.

It was only after the government had started to challenge the most vexing aspects of regional specialization, its status as the centre of labour-intensive and low-wage industry, that the ethnic division of labour came to attract attention. There emerged a general desire, now identified with the nationalist movement, to put an end to the separate domains which had been historically attributed to the English and to the French. Quebec politics came to be overwhelmingly concerned with ending the age-old division between economic and cultural life.

From that point on it became impossible to avoid a direct confrontation with Montreal's English-speaking community, which was certainly not disposed to give up the benefits resulting from its historical role as manager of the economy. It was not prepared to share the remunerative and stimulating jobs which it could automatically count on at the head of the large corporate bureaucracies based in Montreal. The bulk of the English-speaking population rallied behind its business leaders in opposing any manifestation of French nationalism, particularly as regards careers, the use of French in head-office operations, and the expansion of provincial power at the expense of federal authority.

Two of the expressions frequently used by Premier René Lévesque in describing his party's goals are "a normal society" and "a complete society." What he means is that the people of Quebec, individually and collectively, should have access to a much wider range of opportunities. This is not radically different from what Premier Peter Lougheed is trying to achieve for Alberta. The royalties derived from the oil and gas industry which have been accumulating in that province's Heritage Fund are meant to ensure that Alberta will be able to build a diversified economic base offering greater security and broader interests and occupations than those available in the past. These goals are shared by other provinces eager for more autonomous economic development.

At the present time Canada is undergoing a transformation which, if not entirely perceptible, is nonetheless very painful. The crisis results from the failure of the traditional economic vision as a principle of social organization. In this sparsely settled country, with its harsh climate and its high costs, social goals have often had to be sacrificed to greater productivity and efficiency. Even the sense of nationhood has had to be played down in order to allow a free hand to foreign capital and technology, which were expected to bring greater material well-being. Indeed, there are few industrialized countries in the world today with such minimal control over their resources, economic institutions, and economic development as has Canada. As a means of promoting its own growth, Canada has consistently sought to preserve a semi-colonial relationship, first with Britain through imperial preference, and then with the United States through various modes of continentalism. The justification for these policies was always an economic one.

Not surprisingly, the social costs have been heavy. The most obvious ones have been the persistence of ethnic stratification and of regional specialization, along with the undemocratic character they both conferred on Canadian politics. At the same time, the country has had to put up with authoritarian businessmen, dissembling politicians, and timorous governments. Its development is noted for overinvestment in national projects and underinvestment in local or regional ones. Correspondingly, the country is more vulnerable than others to the twin problems of inflation and unemployment.

The question now is whether Canada's political structures can be adapted to a new situation or whether they must give way to a new type of relationship between its constituent regions. It is apparent that new values will replace the economic rationality that played such a large role in Canadian history but which now seems incapable of coping with present needs. It will become necessary to formulate economic policy in such a way that it is compatible with popular and regional expectations. In other words, economic notions of progress and development will have to be subordinated to newer social ones.

Current trends might be expected to ease the tensions which have come to a head between English and French, along with the intergovernmental and bureaucratic rivalries between Ottawa and Quebec. The historical opposition of the French to the prevailing economic system would lose a great deal of its relevance in a context where social values had precedence over purely economic ones. Similarly, it would become easier to reconcile national policies with the way in which the French have always perceived their own needs and their own goals. However, the past is not so easily done away with. It is almost impossible to ignore the extent to which 200 years of English and French interaction have shaped attitudes and behaviours.

Yet the success with which Canada is able to make the transition to a new type of society will depend to a large degree on the accommodations English and French are able to achieve within Quebec and on the way each group is able to see itself in a diversified and pluralistic society. The reason why Quebec is so important in the present context is that Canada's political and economic system will not function properly without the concurrence of the French population in that province.

There is among the French a historical tempta-
tion to fall back on a closed system that rejects outside
influence and seeks to impose a stifling form of
homogeneity. The risk there is that the French-
speaking population of Quebec may not be strong
enough to maintain by itself a flourishing culture in
the North American context. As for the English-
speaking community, which is experiencing enormous
difficulties in adjusting to a new role, it must avoid the
slow death that could result from an excessive rigidity
on the part of its leaders.

The Trojan Horse

In 1977, when Quebec's National Assembly adopted Bill 101, there was a euphoric feeling among the French that at last the survival of their language and culture had been ensured. New immigrants would be forced to integrate into the French community instead of being allowed to gravitate towards the English one. The English language would lose a great deal of its attraction at work and in the marketplace. There was a general conviction that the traditional French culture of Quebec would be able to express itself freely and that it would henceforth dominate the social and economic environment.

Yet, in less than two years, Bill 101 began to take on the look of a Trojan horse: not only would French Quebec be called upon to make room for thousands of newcomers, but it would also have to undergo profound changes itself as a result of their arrival. At the very moment when French collective identity seems assured, it is called upon to transform itself: Vietnamese, Greek, and Portuguese immigrants are bringing to Quebec their own values and attitudes and will be seeking recognition for them from the French. The monolithic character of French society, largely derived from its minority status in Canada, will have to become pluralistic in the light of the majority status it is asserting within Quebec.

The Parti Québécois' language legislation, designed to curb the growth of the English community, also caused French society to open up in a way that is without precedent, except perhaps for the acceptance of industrialization in the decade that followed the Rebellion of 1837. This important aspect of the law, however, is taking some time to penetrate the political consciousness of the French majority. Indeed, it was completely ignored in the deluge of documents and speeches which preceded adoption of the law. The possibility that French society might be profoundly influenced by immigrants it was forcibly integrating did not even cross the minds of the sociologists, civil servants, and politicians who drafted the legislation.

Such a blind spot may be attributed to the recurring preoccupation of French society over the last 200 years with seeking some form of protective isolation from the outside world, that is, from the English, from immigrants, and from foreign ideas. Consequently, most French-speaking people in the province are unaware of the impact which immigration has had on North America, and they do not realize the extent to which the dominant Anglo-Protestant culture has changed under the impact of these newcomers.

Unlike most other North American communities, French Quebec has not experienced this process of cultural accommodation which is now an accepted dimension of life in New York, Boston, San Francisco, and also in English Montreal. About ten years ago, however, Quebec began to feel the first restless stirrings of ethnic groups when the provincial government set up its own immigration department and developed an aggressive policy to serve Quebec's cultural priorities. Recruiting offices were opened in various parts of the world in order to attract immigrants who were either French-speaking or who could be expected to fit in without too many language difficulties. But during this period of intense nationalism, French society remained inward-looking and uninterested in newcomers. Public institutions, expecting immigrants to assimilate without any trouble, made little effort to welcome them and help them adapt to their new situation. Schools, hospitals, unions, and the public service remained aloof in spite of the friendliness usually displayed by individual Quebecers.

Twenty or thirty years ago the dominant Anglo-Protestant group in Canada and in the United States also insisted on rapid assimilation and cultural conformity. But this attitude is no longer tenable, simply because of the growing political power displayed by ethnic groups. The best example of the concessions they have been able to wrench from the society around them is the affirmative-action legislation in the United States which offers under-represented groups such as Puerto Ricans, Blacks, and women better protection and support on the labour market.

The linguistic model which French society is attempting to recreate for itself within Quebec is the Canadian model of the period before the 1960s, according to which the various ethnic groups accepted their own subordination to a majority group and readily adapted to the stratification and specialization imposed on the labour market. However, Quebec minorities have already developed a strong sense of their cultural rights. Ever since the St. Leonard school crisis of 1968, ethnic groups have been the object of linguistic competition between French and English institutions such as schools and hospitals. This painful experience has toughened their resolve to find a proper place for themselves in Quebec, particularly as Bill 101 established in no uncertain terms that they would have to make their peace with French society. Accordingly, immigrants are easily accepting the use of French, which they see simply as another means of communication.

Education is turning out to be one of the most sensitive issues between the French majority and the ethnic minorities in Montreal. Following the adoption of Bill 101 in 1977, a large number of immigrant children enrolled in French schools, which with very few exceptions belong to the Catholic confessional system. Many parents—Sephardic Jews from North Africa, Vietnamese, Indians, and Pakistanis—had little affinity for the religious traditions which still prevail in the province's French public schools. They requested that their children be exempted from religious education. In some schools where they happened to be in a majority the local parents' association applied for a change in the institution's confessional status. At Notre-Dame-des-Neiges School in Montreal, non-Christian parents seemed to be successful, having received government approval and engaged in a long court wrangle, until the Montreal Catholic School Commission decided that it would not operate non-confessional schools. The issue is still unresolved and it has left the parents in a legal no-man's-land.

Historically the school system has played a key role in preserving the homogeneity of the French society in Quebec. Immigrants whose language and religion differed from that of the majority were pushed towards the Anglo-Protestant system, whose resistance, as in the case of Jews, was overcome by means of direct political pressures or simply by legislative intervention. Therefore, as English schools, both Anglo-Protestant and Anglo-Catholic, began to exhibit unprecedented cultural diversity, French schools remained the leading centres of resistance to pluralism.

French Catholics in Montreal constitute an extremely powerful lobby that has thwarted government plans to unite the city's confessional school systems into a more efficient and economical organization whose division would be along language lines. In the 1977 elections to the Montreal Catholic School Commission, a slate of Catholic candidates handily defeated another one made up of Parti Québécois militants and sympathizers.

The strength displayed by Catholics in local school elections does not stem solely from a resurgence of religious sentiment. It is largely related to a form of social conservatism, an attachment to traditional values of which the most important is the preservation of parental authority over decisions affecting the future of their children. Catholic lobbying and electioneering is part of the resistance to the centralizing and socializing tendencies of government and it seeks to promote local and parental control over schools and school boards. Catholics are in effect challenging the growing power of the state and of the bureaucracy over their lives.

Ethnic groups have also been pressing for changes in the educational system to obtain recognition of Quebec's multicultural character. They want the French system to reflect the growing ethnic and religious diversity of the province, particularly in the composition of the teaching staff, the pedagogical materials employed, and the educational programs being enforced. The urgency of these reforms is illustrated by the plight of Haitian children enrolled in French schools. A large number of them have been placed in slow-learner classes simply because local school boards are failing to take important social and cultural facts into account in evaluating and teaching these children.

Over the past ten years more than 18,000 Haitians have come to Quebec, and about 4,000 children are in school. These children enter the educational system knowing Creole but little French. Nevertheless, the schools consider Haiti a French-speaking country and will not accept the idea that Haitian children have to be placed in special language classes for newcomers. School boards are also ignoring the fact that the students' previous training in Haiti was generally very weak in mathematics and science.

Instead of taking remedial action, authorities are simply relegating the students to slow-learner classes. Another factor working against Haitian children is the permissive atmosphere in the classrooms, to which they find it difficult to adapt after the disciplined Haitian system.

The network of social services is another area which the ethnic minorities want to reshape according to their cultural and linguistic needs. At the present time, the focus is on the neighbourhood-based Local Community Service Centres in areas of Montreal where there are large concentrations of immigrants. These parapublic agencies are important to ethnic groups because they serve as entry points for the whole range of welfare and health services. In 1979, just as a group of immigrant parents were challenging the confessional status of Notre-Dame-des-Neiges School, a group of social workers were establishing a common front whose aim was to bring about changes in the language policy of public institutions in Quebec.

The problems of St. Louis ward in Montreal illustrate the kind of situation these social workers had in mind. The area is the first stop for newly arrived immigrants who provide cheap labour for some 500 garment and textile sweatshops in the centre of the city. They often come from poor villages in Portugal, Italy, and Greece, and they face great difficulties in adapting to industrial employment and urban life in Montreal. Many of them never manage to learn French or English and are helpless when confronted with the bureaucratic complexity of unemployment insurance, welfare, health services, and the educational system. Yet they have trouble obtaining counselling in their own language when faced with unmanageable personal problems.

Although Quebec receives about 25,000 immigrants a year, the social affairs department has done very little for them in programs, staff, or funding. In fact, the government opposes the idea of serving immigrants in their own language and making allowances for their cultural differences. Civil servants and their unions are also displaying considerable opposition to the idea of providing services in a language other than French. For example, the Office de la langue française—the board that oversees the francization of industry and acts as a language watchdog—joined the union representing the staff of the St. Louis Local Community Service Centre in opposing advertising for a Chinese-speaking nurse for the local Chinese population. In their view, French-only services are adequate and it is not necessary to hire staff with ethnic backgrounds.

Poor participation in the provincial public service is another sore point with English-speaking people and with ethnic groups. Their combined representation at the end of 1979 was less than 3 per cent, which is far below their combined strength of about 20 per cent in the over-all population. But it is only lately that non-French elements have become aware of the disadvantages of poor representation in the public service in terms of jobs, services, and influence.

Because the provincial government had been perceived historically as the government of the French, there was little interest in the career opportunities that opened up after 1960 as a result of the expansion of the bureaucracy. The French were given a virtual monopoly of jobs in that sector, most of them in the relatively remote and unilingual provincial capital. English and ethnic minorities began showing interest in public-service jobs only when the migration of head office and research functions resulted in a shrinking job market, and when the regionalization of the Canadian economy gave the French language a greater value than it had ever had before.

French resistance to diversifying the composition of the provincial public service stems mainly from the feeling that it is a vital institution in the struggle against the historical attempts of the federal government to expand its own powers and jurisdiction. Moreover, there is also the unstated view that it is fitting for the provincial service to be solely French, given the resolutely English character of large national corporations which severely limits career opportunities for French-speaking people. In this situation it is rather difficult for Montreal's English population and for ethnic groups to gain more than token recognition.

In effect, the French in Quebec are reproducing in their own language the nation-building process that took place earlier in English Canada. This process was based on the enforcement of a linguistically homogeneous environment, on policies of assimilation, and on the exclusion of elements that did not readily integrate into the mainstream. It resulted, for instance, in the abrogation of French language and educational rights. The difficulty of adopting a more pluralistic view of society is illustrated by the hesitations of English-speaking provinces about the use of French in the courts and by their refusal to accept French school boards with independent taxation powers.

The nation-building efforts of the French majority in Quebec are a source of great anxiety and frustration for all those who do not share its collective goals. The effects of the changes which have taken place over the last twenty years, which have accelerated in the last five, are analogous to the unsettling social impact of inflation. There has been a dramatic shift of economic power into the hands of a new group which is untested and viewed with deep misgivings. The changes in Quebec society are causing a rapid obsolescence of certain professional skills and making insatiable demands for new ones. This is causing a rapid shuffling of social classes and values. Some groups are being propelled upwards and they view the future with confidence. Others are given to a kind of collective depression as they see their own situation

rapidly deteriorating without visible means of redress.

The problem faced by a large proportion of the
ethnic population of Montreal is that, having once
made the painful adaptation to an English-dominated
economy, they must now repeat the whole process
again. They must integrate into an economy which in
time will become exclusively French.

The Jewish minority has spent generations
patiently trying to overcome the active discrimination
of the Anglo-Protestant business world. Today,
residual anti-semitism is almost inconsequential and is
limited mainly to older financial institutions, such as
banks. Otherwise there are few career limitations
applying to Jews. English community institutions,
hospitals, school boards, and universities have opened
up and recognized the important Jewish contributions
to the English-speaking community as a whole. But at
the very moment when they have seemingly found
complete acceptance within the English community,
the French began to threaten the social and economic
gains achieved by the Jews—not through anti-
semitism, but through nationalist attacks on the
status of the English language.

It is the English community proper which is
finding the new situation most disorienting. It is called
upon to give up its pre-eminent role in the provincial
economy and to accept the end of the domain which
history had assigned to it. Nationalist attacks on the
use of the English language are particularly disturbing because they constitute an assault on its cultural
identity in a way that is not applicable to Jews and
other minority groups.

Implementation of the Parti Québécois' language
legislation adopted in 1977 has raised two crucial
political issues. The more obvious one is whether the
English community in Montreal can be expected to
survive indefinitely as immigrants are cut off from
access to English schools, as out-migration keeps

thinning its ranks, and as the language of business becomes predominantly French. The second question, which the French majority still has to ask itself, is how the French community will handle the pressures of English-speaking people and of ethnic groups for political and economic equality.

The most critical problem facing the English community in Montreal has to do with the attitudes of the French majority. Nationalist elements tend to believe that the main obstacle in the way of a balanced and prosperous French society is the preponderant economic and cultural influence of English Canada and of the United States. There is a persistent effort to reduce that influence. There may actually be a fair degree of hostility within the Parti Québécois towards the English; the bulk of the population, although not sharing this sentiment, feels that there is a cultural and social struggle in progress from whose continuation it confidently expects to benefit.

The English community has been much weakened by the exodus of head offices and of managerial and research functions. It can no longer rely on business spokesmen for its defence, nor can it count on the protective influence of the federal government, the balance of power having shifted to the provinces in cultural matters. One positive factor, however, is the community's close identification with the majority language of Canada and of the United States, which helps prevent total isolation.

Twenty years ago English community institutions were still largely self-financing. With increasing reliance on provincial funds, French politicians and bureaucrats came to have an important say in the way these would operate, and even whether individual institutions would continue or not. But the French population at large has come to play a crucial role in this regard. Its views on the English, on the development of pluralism within its own community and society, must now be taken into account. In the past, its acceptance of the English community was based mostly on the latter's economic, managerial, and technological contribution to Quebec. This role which has now been challenged by the French must be replaced by something else if the English community is not to be slowly eroded by rejection and by financial starvation as were the French communities in many parts of Canada.

In effect, this means that English community institutions must justify their existence in the eyes of the French population, which has the final say in the disposal of taxation revenues. They must carve out a role for themselves which is acceptable to the majority and which is perceived to have some usefulness for the province as a whole. This constitutes a dramatic transformation in outlook for the self-contained and culturally autonomous English-speaking population of Montreal. The change is not willingly and spontaneously accepted. It requires an ability to mingle and work with the French in a quite different manner, without the condescension that existed before the Quiet Revolution. The new situation places considerable emphasis on personal initiative and flexibility, particularly among those in managerial positions. It requires the ability to convince French counterparts of the general usefulness of the English contribution to Quebec.

But if there is to be any breakthrough in the direction of a pluralistic French society it will have to be achieved mainly as a result of the efforts of the ethnic minorities. As the third force in provincial politics, one that has steadily been gaining in numerical importance, they are in a far better position than anyone else to make claims on the French majority and to wrest concessions from which the English will ultimately benefit. They are no longer identified with competition for low-paying jobs, nor are they associated with English domination of the provincial economy. Their ability to influence election results in several ridings of Montreal makes it more than likely that, once politicized and mobilized, they will be able to secure some profound changes in Quebec's cultural policies and attitudes.

The linguistic and cultural compromises that will be realized over the next few years in the Montreal area, where most of the English and ethnic population of Quebec happens to be concentrated, will ultimately determine the manner in which the French majority considers its relations with the rest of Canada. The ability to deal with internal problems will eventually affect external relations. Hence, the constitutional debates on renewed federalism, on sovereignty-association, and on outright separation will remain unresolved until some equilibrium has been reached between the French, the English, and the ethnic minorities within the province. Until then Canada will continue to experience the same uncertainty it has known for the last ten years or so.

Notes

Chapter 1

1. Quoted by Fernand Ouellet in *Histoire économique et sociale du Québec, 1760-1850* (Montreal: Fides, 1966), p. 7.
2. *Lord Durham's Report: An Abridgement of "Report on the Affairs of British North America,"* ed. Gerald M. Craig (Toronto: McClelland and Stewart, Carleton Library, 1963), p. 28.
3. Ibid., p. 150.
4. Ibid., p. 149.
5. Ibid., p. 31.

Chapter 2

1. Durham, pp. 30-31.
2. Ibid., pp. 79.

Chapter 3

1. Marcel Rioux, *Quebec in Question*, trans. James Boake (Toronto: James Lorimer, 1971).
2. For a fuller discussion of this idea, see R. N. Morris and C. M. Lanphier, *Three Scales of Inequality* (Toronto: Longman Canada, 1977).
3. See Hannah Arendt's discussion of "the rights of Englishmen" versus "the rights of man" in Hannah Arendt, *The Origins of Totalitarianism*, part 2, *Imperialism* (New York: Harcourt, Brace and World, 1951), p. 175.
4. Claude-Armand Sheppard, *Inventaire critique des droits linguistiques au Québec*, study for the Commission of Inquiry on the Position of the French Language and on Language Rights in Quebec (Quebec: Editeur officiel du Québec, 1973), p. 11.

5. Rioux, p. 120. By mistake Simms is referred to as Simons.
6. Wallace Clement, *Continental Corporate Power* (Toronto: McClelland and Stewart, 1977), p. 257.

Chapter 4

1. Emile Gosselin, "L'Administration publique dans un pays bilingue et biculturel," *Canadian Public Administration* 6 (1963): 411.
2. Mason Wade, *The French Canadians, 1760-1967* (Toronto: Macmillan, 1968), p. 93.
3. Claude-Armand Sheppard, *The Law of Languages in Canada*, Studies of the Royal Commission on Bilingualism and Biculturalism, no. 10 (Ottawa: Government of Canada, 1971), p. 48.
4. Thomas Chapais, *Cours d'histoire du Canada*, 8 vols. (Montreal: Editions Bernard Valiquette, 1919-1934), 2: 69.
5. Wade, p. 103 (our italics).
6. Durham, p. 151.
7. Chapais, 5: 83.
8. Durham, p. 149.
9. Ramsay Cook, *Canada and the French-Canadian Question* (Toronto: Macmillan, 1966), p. 38.
10. Ibid., p. 39.
11. Guy Bouthillier and Jean Meynaud, *Le Choc des langues au Québec, 1760-1970* (Montreal: Les Presses de l'Université du Québec, 1972), p. 34.
12. For further details, see ibid., p. 326.
13. For further details, see ibid., pp. 563-66.

Chapter 6

1. Bill 62, introduced in 1969, was one of three controversial bills introduced by various governments to streamline the Montreal school system. Others were Bill 28 in 1971 and Bill 71 in 1972, which was the only one to become law.
2. See Dominique Clift, "Language Use among Montreal's Working Population," *Montreal Star*, 27 March-2 April

1976. This study showed that 33 per cent of English workers in Montreal were in administrative and professional occupations compared with only 18 per cent of French workers. See also *Report of the Commission of Inquiry on the Position of the French Language and on Language Rights in Quebec*, book 1, *Language of Work* (Quebec: Editeur officiel du Québec, 1972), p. 78, table 1.40. (Hereafter cited as *Language of Work*.) This table shows that in Quebec a majority of the English and a minority of the French work for large corporations.

3. This idea is explored in Pierre Beaulieu, *Montreal Organizations and Bill 62 and Bill 28: An Analysis of Their Ideological Approaches* (Montreal: Montreal Island School Council, 1975), and in Pierre Fournier, "A Political Analysis of School Reorganization in Montreal" (MA thesis, McGill University, 1971).

4. See *Language of Work*, p. 17, table 1.3. This shows that in Quebec 216,000 unilingual anglophones force 637,000 francophones to work in English. There are a total of 1,820,000 French-speaking workers and 344,000 English-speaking workers.

5. According to Clift, "Language Use among Montreal's Working Population," 15 per cent of all English workers in the Montreal area were enrolled in French courses.

6. See *Language of Work*, p. 37, table 1.70. According to the English business elite, francization would be practicable only at the clerical and blue-collar levels (p. 132, table 1.69).

7. J. MacNamara and J. Edwards, *Attitudes to Learning French in English-speaking Schools in Quebec*, Report of the Commission of Inquiry on the Position of the French Language and on Language Rights in Quebec, study 7 (Quebec: Editeur officiel du Québec, 1973).

8. See Clift, "Language Use among Montreal's Working Population."

9. Kathleen Connors, N. Ménard, and R. Singh, "Testing Linguistic and Functional Competence in Immersion Programs," in *Aspects of Bilingualism*, ed. Michel

Paradis (Columbia, S.C.: Hornbeam Press, 1979), pp. 65-75.

10. Gary Cziko et al., "Graduates of Early Immersion," in *The Social and Psychological Context of Language*, ed. Robert St. Clair and Howard Giles (Hillsdale, N.J.: Lawrence Erlbaum Associates, 1979). Other important publications which explore the relationship between environment and second-language learning are: G. Bibeau, *Report of the Independent Study on the Language Training Programmes of the Public Service of Canada* (Ottawa: Public Service of Canada, 1976); Alison d'Anglejan, "Language Learning in and out of Classrooms," in *Understanding Foreign and Second Language Learning*, ed. J. Richards (Rawley, Mass.: Newbury House, 1978); J. MacNamara, J. Svarc, and S. Horner, "Attending a Primary School of the Other Language in Montreal," in *The Bilingual Child* (New York: Academic Press, 1976); I. Spilka, "Assessment of Second Language Performance," *Canadian Modern Language Review* 5 (1976): 543-62.

11. Gary Caldwell, *Out-Migration of English Mother-Tongue High School Leavers from Quebec, 1971-76* (Lennoxville: Anglo Québec en Mutation Committee, 1976).

Chapter 10

1. See Jeremy Boissevain, *The Italians of Montreal* (Ottawa: Royal Commission on Bilingualism and Biculturalism, Government of Canada, 1971), p. 15.

2. For a more detailed discussion of this, see Wade, p. 864, and Paul Cappon, *Conflit entre les néo-Canadiens et les francophones de Montréal* (Quebec: Les Presses de l'Université Laval, 1974), pp. 35-39.

Bibliographic Essays

Historical Background

It is impossible to grasp the nature of English-French relations in Quebec without knowing the economic history of Canada. For this reason, we relied extensively upon historians who describe the links between geography, climate, economic development, and the nature of the elites of the population. One of these is Donald Creighton, who in *The Empire of the St. Lawrence* commented that from the earliest days of Quebec the St. Lawrence was clearly "the destined pathway of North American trade" and that "from the river there arose, like an exhalation, the dream of a western commercial empire." The river, he wrote, "was to be the basis of a great transportation system by which the manufactures of the old world could be exchanged for the staple products of the new." In Creighton's view, the St. Lawrence River profoundly influenced economic development and political behaviour.

Many other historians accept this view about the St. Lawrence, although they do not necessarily share Creighton's admiration for the English merchants of the nineteenth century or his thinly veiled aversion to the French population. Stanley Ryerson in *Unequal Union* describes Confederation as a financial manoeuvre designed to extend the empire of the St. Lawrence through construction of the railway. Tom Naylor in *The History of Canadian Business 1867-1914* meticulously documents the collusion between business and government which was always a characteristic of the system. Lord Durham, whom no one would suspect of precocious Marxism, was one of the first to identify this as a problem. He attributed the pitiable state of Upper Canada at the beginning of the nineteenth century to the Family Compact, which was the name given to the illegitimate union of political authority and economic leadership. Looking at recent history, Pierre Fournier in *The Quebec Establishment* examines the links between government and business in Quebec from the Quiet Revolution until 1974.

The interaction between English economy and French society, as well as the debate on the seigneurial system, is described by Creighton and by Fernand Ouellet in his *Histoire économique et sociale du Québec, 1760-1850*. Mason Wade was an important source on general history as was Lionel Groulx on ideological development.

Three authors were particularly valuable on English-French relations: Ramsay Cook on the status of the two founding peoples since Confederation; Richard Joy on the polarization of language groups today; and Richard Jones on social changes in Quebec and their effects on the two principal language groups. *French-Canadian Society*, edited by Marcel Rioux and Yves Martin, was very useful, particularly the section on economic structure and social stratification with its articles by Albert Faucher, Maurice Lamontagne, Jacques Brazeau, Jacques Dofny, Guy Rocher, and Marcel Rioux.

Donald Creighton. *The Empire of the St. Lawrence*. Toronto: Macmillan, 1956.

Stanley Ryerson. *Unequal Union: Roots of the Crisis in the Canadas, 1815-1873*. Toronto, Progress Books, 1973.

Tom Naylor. *The History of Canadian Business 1867-1914*. Toronto: James Lorimer, 1975.

_____. "The Rise and Fall of the Third Commercial Empire of the St. Lawrence in Canada." In *Canada: A Sociological Profile*, edited by W. E. Mann and Les Wheatcroft. Toronto: Copp Clark, 1976.

Lord Durham [John George Lambton]. *Lord Durham's Report: An Abridgement of "Report on the Affairs of British North America."* Edited by Gerald M. Craig. Toronto: McClelland and Stewart, Carleton Library, 1963.

Pierre Fournier. *The Quebec Establishment.* Montreal: Black Rose Books, 1976.

Fernand Ouellet. *Histoire économique et sociale du Québec, 1760-1850.* Montreal: Fides, 1966.

————. "Les Fondements historiques de l'option séparatiste dans le Québec." *Canadian Historical Review* 43 (3 September 1962).

————, ed. *Papineau, textes choisis.* Quebec: Les Presses de l'Université Laval, 1970.

Mason Wade. *The French Canadians, 1760-1967.* Toronto: Macmillan, 1968.

Lionel Groulx. *Histoire du Canada français depuis la découverte.* Montreal: Fides, 1960.

Thomas Chapais. *Cours d'histoire du Canada.* 8 vols. Montreal: Editions Bernard Valiquette, 1919-1934.

Michel Brunet. *Canadians et Canadiens.* Montreal: Fides, 1954.

————. *La Présence anglaise et les Canadiens.* Montreal: Beauchemin, 1958.

————. "The British Conquest and the Canadiens." *Canadian Historical Review* 40 (2 June 1959).

Jean Hamelin. *Economie et société en Nouvelle-France.* Quebec: Les Presses de l'Université Laval, 1960.

Ramsay Cook. *Canada and the French-Canadian Question.* Toronto: Macmillan, 1966.

Richard Joy. *Languages in Conflict.* Toronto: McClelland and Stewart, 1972.

————. *Canada's Official-Language Minorities.* Montreal: C. D. Howe Research Institute, 1978.

Richard Jones. *Community in Crisis.* Toronto: McClelland and Stewart, 1972.

Marcel Rioux and Yves Martin, eds. *French-Canadian Society.* Toronto: McClelland and Stewart, 1971.

The Language Conflict

The chapters on language were very much influenced by the concept of language and domains as explored by American sociolinguist Joshua Fishman in his writings on the relationship between language, nationalism, and modernization. Fishman is especially interested in societies where groups use different languages in particular domains. In Quebec, English was the language of business while French prevailed in politics and culture. This system works, notes Fishman, as long as the status and powers of the groups in question remain the same. However, language conflicts tend to appear when industrialization, democratization, and modernization modify the relationship between the groups.

Documentation on language use and collective vocations in Canada can be found in a number of studies starting with those commissioned by the Royal Commission on Bilingualism and Biculturalism. *The Work World*, published in 1969, looks at the relationship between occupations, socio-economic status, and language in the business milieu in Montreal and in the federal civil service. Another important source is the *Language of Work* volume of the Commission of Inquiry on the Position of the French Language and on Language Rights in Quebec, published in 1972. More recent changes in the social climate in Quebec as well as shifts in behaviour and attitudes are reflected in Dominique Clift's "Language Use Among Montreal's Working Population" published in the *Montreal Star* in 1976. Two other writers who look at the dynamics behind today's changing language domains are sociologists Hubert Guindon and Jacques Brazeau.

The English community opposed the breakdown of the historic domains and the legislation that was designed to make French the language of business. This is clearly shown in a special analysis prepared by Pierre Beaulieu for the Montreal Island School Council on the attitudes of the English community to school reorganization proposals. Two other revealing studies on the question focus upon French immersion programs in English schools. The first by Connors et al. looks at the success of French immersion programs from the point of view of French language fluency; the second by Cziko et al. examines attitudes of French immersion graduates and their parents to the French community.

The latter two studies deal with the question of social context and second-language learning. Important work in this area has been done by D'Anglejan, Bibeau, Spilka, and MacNamara, who show that languages cannot be properly learned outside the environment where they are regularly spoken. Attitudes to the French community and to the status of French also play an important role in learning the second language. In Montreal considerable work on this issue has been done over the past ten years by a group of social psychologists, most of whom are at McGill University. These include Wallace Lambert, R. C. Gardner, and G. R. Tucker.

For general historical background on the language question three sources were useful: Claude-Armand Sheppard's *The Law of Languages in Canada*, Guy Bouthillier and Jean Meynaud's *Le Choc des langues au Québec, 1760-1970*, and André Dufour's *La Législation récente en matière linguistique dans les provinces d'Ontario, du Manitoba et du Nouveau-Brunswick*.

Joshua Fishman. *The Sociology of Language*. Rawley, Mass.: Newbury House, 1972.

_____. "Domains and the Relationship between Micro- and Macro-sociolinguistics." In *Directions in Sociolinguistics: The Ethnography of Communication*, edited by J. J. Gumperz and D. Hymes. New York: Holt, Rinehart and Winston, 1972.

————. "Sociolinguistics and the Language Problems of Developing Countries." In *Language Problems of Developing Nations*, edited by Joshua Fishman. New York: John Wiley, 1968.

Stanley Lieberson. "A Societal Theory of Race and Ethnic Relations." *American Sociological Review* 26 (1961).

Royal Commission on Bilingualism and Biculturalism. *Report of the Royal Commission on Bilingualism and Biculturalism*, vol. 3, *The Work World*. Ottawa: Government of Canada, 1969.

Commission of Inquiry on the Position of the French Language and on Language Rights in Quebec. *Report of the Commission of Inquiry on the Position of the French Language and on Language Rights in Quebec*, vol. 1, *Language of Work*. Quebec: Editeur officiel du Québec, 1972.

Dominique Clift. "Language Use Among Montreal's Working Population." *Montreal Star*, 27 March-2 April 1976.

Hubert Guindon. "Modernization of Quebec and the Legitimacy of the Canadian State." In *Modernization and the Canadian State*, edited by Daniel Glenday, Allan Turowetz, and Hubert Guindon. Toronto: Macmillan, 1978.

Jacques Brazeau. "Les Incidences psycho-sociologiques de la langue de travail sur l'individu." In *Le Français langue de travail*, edited by Jacques Brazeau et al. Quebec: Les Presses de l'Université Laval, 1971.

Everett C. Hughes. *French Canada in Transition*. Chicago: University of Chicago Press, 1943.

Christopher Beattie. *Minority Men in a Majority Setting*. Toronto: McClelland and Stewart, 1975.

Stanley Lieberson. *Language and Ethnic Relations in Canada*. New York: John Wiley, 1970.

John Jackson. "The Function of Language in Canada." In *The Individual, Language and Society*, edited by W. H. Coons, Donald M. Taylor, and Marc-Adélard Tremblay. Ottawa: Canada Council, 1978.

Pierre Beaulieu. *Montreal Organizations and Bill 62 and Bill 28: An Analysis of Their Ideological Approaches*. Montreal: Montreal Island School Council, 1975.

J. P. Proulx. *La Communauté montréalaise et la restructuration scolaire*. Montreal: Montreal Island School Council, 1975.

Kathleen Connors, N. Ménard, and R. Singh. "Testing Linguistic and Functional Competence in Immersion Programs." In *Aspects of Bilingualism*, edited by Michel Paradis. Columbia, S.C.: Hornbeam Press, 1978.

Gary Cziko, Wallace E. Lambert, Nelly Sidoti, and Richard Tucker. "Graduates of Early Immersion: Retrospective Views of Grade 11 Students and their Parents." In *The Social and Psychological Context of Language*, edited by Robert St. Clair and Howard Giles. Hillsdale, N.J.: Lawrence Erlbaum Associates, 1979.

Alison d'Anglejan. "Language Learning in and out of Classrooms." In *Understanding Foreign and Second Language Learning*, edited by J. Richards. Rawley, Mass.: Newbury House, 1978.

G. Bibeau. *Report of the Independent Study on the Language Training Programmes of the Public Service of Canada*. Ottawa: Public Service of Canada, 1976.

I. Spilka. "Assessment of Second Language Performance." *Canadian Modern Language Review* 5 (1976): 543-62.

J. MacNamara, J. Svarc, and S. Horner. "Attending a Primary School of the Other Language in Montreal." In *The Bilingual Child*. New York: Academic Press, 1976.

W. E. Lambert et al. "A Study of the Roles of Attitudes and Motivation in Second Language Learning." In *Readings in the Sociology of Language*, edited by J. A. Fishman. The Hague: Mouton, 1968.

W. E. Lambert. "A Social Psychology of Bilingualism." *Journal of Social Issues*, April 1967.

R. C. Gardner and W. E. Lambert. "Motivational Variables in Second Language Acquisition." *Canadian Journal of Psychology* (1959).

W. E. Lambert, R. C. Gardner, H. C. Barik, and K. Tunstall. "Attitudinal and Cognitive Aspects of Intensive Study of a Second Language." *Journal of Abnormal and Social Psychology* (1963).

G. R. Tucker and H. Gadalof. "Bilinguals as Linguistic Mediators." In *Readings in Introductory Psycholinguistics*, edited by G. Richard Tucker. New York: Simon and Schuster, 1973.

Claude-Armand Sheppard. *The Law of Languages in Canada*. Studies of the Royal Commission on Bilingualism and Biculturalism, no. 10. Ottawa: Government of Canada, 1971.

Guy Bouthillier and Jean Meynaud. *Le Choc des langues au Québec, 1760-1970*. Montreal: Les Presses de l'Université du Québec, 1972.

André Dufour. *La Législation récente en matière linguistique dans les provinces d'Ontario, du Manitoba et du Nouveau-Brunswick*. Study E2, Report of the Commission of Inquiry on the Position of the French Language and on Language Rights in Quebec. Quebec: Editeur officiel du Québec, 1973.

Individual and Collective Rights

The notions associated with individual and collective rights are controversial and depend very much upon the area of discussion. In analysing the attachment of the English community to individual rights, we considered two related philosophical traditions: classical liberalism and Protestantism. Among the authors who contributed to the spread of liberalism were Adam Smith, Jeremy Bentham, and James Mill. Max Weber and R. H. Tawney were indispensable sources on the subject of Protestantism.

Liberalism and Protestantism have evolved over the past two centuries to recognize the need for social controls and collective goals. However, thinking in the English community of Montreal remained in the nineteenth century in these fields largely because the English elite identified almost entirely with the economy and veered naturally toward conservatism.

In contrast to the English, the idea of collective rights has always played a role in French thinking and can be found in French social critics such as Jean-Jacques Rousseau who celebrated the "volonté générale" or the "general will" in his *Social Contract* in the eighteenth century, and in sociologist Emile Durkheim who talked about "la solidarité sociale" or "organic solidarity" in his writings a century and a half later.

In the twentieth century, Anglo-Saxon countries recognized the existence of certain collective rights in the fields of unionization and access to education, for example, and aggressive individualism lost much of its relevance. These social rights, as they were called, had little to do with collective rights as understood in Quebec because they were not related to ethnicity. Nevertheless, they contributed to promotion of the group rights idea. An important source for this was T. H. Marshall's *Citizenship and Social Class*.

Collective rights became an issue after World War I when national minorities sought protection under special League of Nations treaties as a result of the new boundaries that were drawn. Hannah Arendt discusses this in *The Origins of Totalitarianism* in the section on imperialism. After that collective rights became associated with ethnicity as minorities all over the world started to make demands upon the states they were living in. The issue faded in the 1940s and 1950s but rose again in the 1960s and 1970s when American minorities, particularly Blacks, demanded different treatment. *Social Justice and Preferential Treatment* by W. T. Blackstone and R. D. Heslep and *Affirmative Discrimination and Public Policy* by Nathan Glazer are two important works on acceptance of collective rights in the United States.

Sources on the situation in Quebec can be found among the special studies commissioned by the Gendron Commission on linguistic rights in Europe and possibilities for their application here. *Three Scales of Inequality* by R. N. Morris and C. M. Lanphier on individual, collective, and cultural rights applies to English-French relations in the general Canadian context.

Henry K. Girvetz. *The Evolution of Liberalism*. Toronto: Collier-Macmillan, 1969.

Adam Smith. *An Inquiry into the Nature and Causes of the Wealth of Nations*. Edited by R. H. Campbell and A. S. Skinner. Oxford: Clarendon Press, 1976.

Max Weber. *The Protestant Ethic and the Spirit of Capitalism*. Translated by Talcott Parsons. New York: Scribner, 1958.

Richard Tawney. *Religion and the Rise of Capitalism*. New York: Harcourt, Brace, 1937.

Philippe Besnard. *Protestantisme et capitalisme: la controverse post-weberienne*. Paris: Colin, 1970.

Jean-Jacques Rousseau. *The Social Contract*. Translated by Maurice Cranston. Baltimore: Penguin Books, 1968.

C. W. Vaughan. *The Political Writings of Jean-Jacques Rousseau*. New York: Wiley, 1962.

Emile Durkheim. *The Division of Labor in Society*. Translated by George Simpson. New York: Free Press of Glencoe, 1964.

T. H. Marshall. *Citizenship and Social Class*. Cambridge: Cambridge University Press, 1950.

Charles W. Eliot. *The Conflict Between Individualism and Collectivism in a Democracy*. Freeport, N.Y.: Books for Libraries Press, 1967.

Hannah Arendt. *The Origins of Totalitarianism*. New York: Harcourt, Brace, 1973.

Nathan Glazer. *Affirmative Discrimination and Public Policy*. New York: Basic Books, 1975.

William T. Blackstone and Robert D. Heslep, eds. *Social Justice and Preferential Treatment: Women and Racial Minorities in Education and Business*. Athens, Ga.: University of Georgia Press, 1977.

Claude-Armand Sheppard. *Inventaire critique des droits linguistiques au Québec*. Study for the Commission of Inquiry on the Position of the French Language and on Language Rights in Quebec. Quebec: Editeur officiel du Québec, 1973.

Jean-Louis Beaudouin and Claude Masse. *Etude comparative et évolutive des droits linguistiques en Belgique et en Suisse*. Study for the Commission of Inquiry on the Position of the French Language and on Language Rights in Quebec. Quebec: Editeur officiel du Québec, 1973.

Gerhard Leibholz. "The Protection of Racial and Linguistic Minorities in Europe during the Nineteenth and Twentieth Centuries." Unpublished monograph for the Commission of Inquiry on the Position of the French Language and on Language Rights in Quebec.

W. J. Ganshof Van der Meersh. "Rapport sur les principes juridiques, idéologiques et historiques relatifs aux droits linguistiques et culturels des minorités linguistiques." Unpublished monograph for the Commission of

Inquiry on the Position of the French Language and on Language Rights in Quebec.

François Chevrette. "Légalité du nombre et légalité du temps: Essai d'analyse des notions de droits des minorités, droits collectifs, droits coutumiers et droits acquis en droit québécois." Unpublished monograph for the Commission of Inquiry on the Position of the French Language and on Language Rights in Quebec.

John Porter. "Ethnic Pluralism in Canadian Perspective." In *Sociology Canada*, edited by Christopher Beattie and Stewart Crysdale. Toronto: Butterworth, 1977.

Raymond N. Morris and C. Michael Lanphier. *Three Scales of Inequality: Perspectives on English-French Relations*. Toronto: Longman Canada, 1977.

Ethnicity

In their book on ethnicity, American social critics Nathan Glazer and Daniel Moynihan comment that in today's world ethnicity has become "a new social category as significant for the understanding of the present-day world as that of social class itself." Fifteen years ago this was not the case. Whether in the United States, Canada, Israel, or the Soviet Union, ethnic groups were marginal peoples who were expected to assimilate and disappear.

Today, however, these ethnic minorities are refusing to assimilate. In addition to retaining their particular cultural identities, they are making claims for power upon the majority cultures. This new approach to ethnicity provides the main orientation for the chapters which touch upon Quebec's cultural communities and the role they are likely to play with the French majority as Quebec evolves.

American sociological literature provides the most important material for this new approach to inter-group relations. The evolution in the writings of Milton Gordon shows how attitudes to the question have changed. In 1964 Gordon produced *Assimilation in American Life*, a clear illustration of the American belief in assimilation. An article in 1975 entitled "Toward a General Theory of Racial and Ethnic Group Relations," however, showed how important pluralism had become.

Other important American sociologists who have studied the growing influence of ethnic groups include Michael Novak, who wrote *The Rise of the Unmeltable Ethnics*; Peter Schrag, who documented the decline of Anglo-Protestant culture in America; and Nathan Glazer and Daniel Moynihan, who studied Blacks, Puerto Ricans, Jews, and Italians in New York City in their book *Beyond the Melting Pot*. S. N. Eisenstadt's work on the absorption of immigrants in Israel and other non-Western countries is also instructive. Three other important authors on the topic are Pierre L. van den Berghe, H. M. Blalock, and R. A. Schermerhorn.

In Canada work in this field is underdeveloped in comparison with the United States. To some extent this is a reflection of the hesitation of Canadians to examine and criticize their own society. Five sociologists who are interested in ethnic stratification and the rise of pluralism are Raymond Breton, Anthony Richmond, David R. Hughes, Evelyn Kallen, and John Porter, author of *The Vertical Mosaic*. This book, now fifteen years old, is still the most comprehensive on the question, although its orientation is in many respects out of date. Porter's article "Ethnic Pluralism in Canadian Perspective" is more reflective of contemporary thinking.

Quebec has even less literature on the changing face of inter-group relations because until recently French society was closed to immigrants and outside influences. Bill 101, however, is forcing Quebec to open up and examine the question of pluralism. Four books which suggest the shape of the conflicts ahead between the French majority and the ethnic groups are Paul Cappon's *Conflit entre les néo-Canadiens et les francophones de Montréal*, Jeremy Boissevain's *The Italians of Montreal*, Paul Dejean's *Les Haïtiens au Québec*, and René Didier and Yvon Bordeleau's *Le Processus des choix linguistiques des immigrants au Québec*. Valuable accounts of Jewish community attitudes can be found in articles by Ruth Wisse, Irwin Cotler, and Michael Yarosky. A useful over-all source book on Quebec immigrants is *Les Groupes ethniques* of the Commission of Inquiry on the Position of the French Language and on Language Rights in Quebec.

Nathan Glazer and Daniel P. Moynihan, eds. *Ethnicity: Theory and Experience*. Cambridge, Mass.: Harvard University Press, 1975.

_____. *Beyond the Melting Pot*. Cambridge, Mass.: Harvard University Press, 1963.

Milton M. Gordon. *Assimilation in American Life*. New York: Oxford University Press, 1964.

_____. "Toward a General Theory of Racial and Ethnic Group Relations." In *Ethnicity: Theory and Experience*, edited by Nathan Glazer and Daniel Moynihan. Cambridge, Mass.: Harvard University Press, 1975.

Michael Novak. *The Rise of the Unmeltable Ethnics*. New York: Macmillan, 1971.

Peter Schrag. *The Decline of the WASP*. New York: Simon and Schuster, 1971.

Shmuel Noah Eisenstadt. *The Absorption of Immigrants*. Westport, Conn.: Greenwood Press, 1975.

Pierre L. van den Berghe. *Race and Racism: A Comparative Perspective*. New York: John Wiley, 1967.

H. M. Blalock, Jr. *Toward a Theory of Minority-Group Relations*. New York: John Wiley, 1967.

R. A. Schermerhorn. *Comparative Ethnic Relations*. New York: Random House, 1970.

Raymond Breton. "Institutional Completeness of Ethnic Communities and the Personal Relations of Immigrants." In *Canadian Society: Sociological Perspectives*, edited by B. R. Blishen et al. Toronto: Macmillan, 1971.

Anthony Richmond. "Immigration and Pluralism in Canada." In *Social and Cultural Change in Canada*, vol. 1, edited by W. E. Mann. Toronto: Copp Clark, 1970.

_____. "Social Mobility of Immigrants in Canada." In *Canadian Society*, edited by B. R. Blishen et al. Toronto: Macmillan, 1971.

David R. Hughes and Evelyn Kallen. *The Anatomy of Racism: Canadian Dimensions*. Montreal: Harvest House, 1974.

M. Kelner. "Ethnic Penetration into Toronto's Elite Structure." *Canadian Review of Sociology and Anthropology* (1970).

Frank G. Valles, Mildred Schwartz, and Frank Darknell. "Ethnic Assimilation and Differentiation in Canada." In *Canadian Society*, edited by B. R. Blishen et al. Toronto: Macmillan, 1971.

Howard Roseborough and Raymond Breton. "Perceptions of the Relative Economic and Political Advantages of Ethnic Groups in Canada." In *Canadian Society*, edited by B. R. Blishen et al. Toronto: Macmillan, 1971.

————. "Ethnic Differences in Status." In *Canadian Society*, edited by B. R. Blishen et al. Toronto: Macmillan, 1971.

John Porter. *The Vertical Mosaic*. Toronto: University of Toronto Press, 1965.

————. "Ethnic Pluralism in Canadian Perspective." In *Sociology Canada*, edited by Christopher Beattie and Stewart Crysdale. Toronto: Butterworth, 1977.

Paul Cappon. *Conflit entre les néo-Canadiens et les francophones de Montréal*. Quebec: Les Presses de l'Université Laval, 1974.

Jeremy Boissevain. *The Italians of Montreal*. Study for the Royal Commission on Bilingualism and Biculturalism. Ottawa: Government of Canada, 1971.

Paul Dejean. *Les Haïtiens au Québec*. Montreal: Les Presses de l'Université du Québec, 1978.

René Didier and Yvon Bordeleau. *Le Processus des choix linguistiques des immigrants au Québec*. Study E6 for the Commission of Inquiry on the Position of the French Language and on Language Rights in Quebec. Quebec: Editeur officiel du Québec, 1973.

Ruth R. Wisse and Irwin Cotler. "Quebec's Jews Caught in the Middle." *Commentary*, September 1977.

Irwin Cotler. "First Encounters: Le Fait Français et le Fait Juif." *Report Magazine*, July/August 1978.

Michael Yarosky. "La Communauté juive dans la société québécoise," translated by Clément Trudel. *Le Devoir*, 20 July 1979.

Commission of Inquiry on the Position of the French Language and on Language Rights in Quebec. *Report of the Commission of Inquiry on the Position of the French Language and on Language Rights in Quebec*, vol. 3, *Ethnic Groups*. Quebec: Editeur officiel du Québec, 1972.

Chronology

1759   Battle of the Plains of Abraham

1763   A Royal Proclamation institutes a policy of assimilation by imposing English law and customs and by excluding Catholics from public office. It also reduces the territory of the former French colony.

1774   The Quebec Act meets the American revolutionary threat by re-establishing French rights and restoring the colony's former borders.

1776   The American Revolution breaks out.

1791   The Constitutional Act divides Canada into two parts and creates elective assemblies, but fails to grant responsible government. The Act inaugurates a period of tension between the executive and the legislative branches of government.

1837   Armed insurrections in Upper and Lower Canada.

1839   Publication of the Durham Report proposing legislative union of Upper and Lower Canada, the granting of responsible government, and the abrogation of the official character of the French language.

1840   The Act of Union implements most of Lord Durham's recommendations.

1848   Faced with an American threat, the Imperial Parliament restores the official use of French.

The British governor sets a precedent by inviting Baldwin and Lafontaine to form a joint cabinet, thereby recognizing the principle of the "double majority" in the Union legislature.

1867   The British North America Act creates modern Canada and recognizes the use of French in Parliament and the courts. It also makes English official in Quebec.

1870   Métis uprising in Manitoba.

1870   The Manitoba Act recognizes English and French as official languages in that province.

1875   The Northwest Territories Act, applying to the future provinces of Saskatchewan and Alberta, recognizes English and French as official languages in the legislature.

1890   Manitoba abrogates the official status of French.

1892   The Northwest Territories abolish the use of French in the legislature.

1910   The Quebec legislature passes a law requiring public utilities to serve customers in French as well as English.

1912   Ontario's Regulation XVII makes English the only teaching language in public schools, thereby eliminating French public education.

1927   First bilingual stamps issued.

1936   Introduction of bilingual currency.

1937   The Union Nationale government under Maurice Duplessis passes a law giving French priority in the interpretation of provincial laws and regulations. Under pressure from the English, the law is abrogated a year later.

1958   Introduction of simultaneous translation in the House of Commons.

1962   The federal government begins to issue bilingual cheques.

1963   Creation of the Royal Commission on Bilingualism and Biculturalism to make recommendations for promoting English-French equality.

1967   Publication of the B & B Report which recommends, among other things, the creation of French units in the federal public service, the establishment of bilingual districts in various areas of Canada, and recognition of the right to education in both English and French.

1968   Riots in the Montreal suburb of St. Leonard as the local Catholic school board eliminates English as a language of education.

1968   Creation of a provincial Commission of Inquiry on the Position of the French Language and on Language Rights in Quebec (the Gendron Commission).

1968   Ontario restores public education in French where the number of students warrants it.

1969   The Quebec government, reacting to the St. Leonard crisis, establishes the principle of freedom of choice for the language of education (Bill 63).

1969   The federal Official Languages Act decrees that all federal services in Ottawa and in certain designated parts of Canada will become available in two languages.

1969   New Brunswick recognizes the official character of English and French in the legislature, in the public service, in education and, where feasible, in the courts.

1970   Manitoba restores French education rights.

1972   The report of the Gendron Commission proposes persuasion to make French the language of work in business and industry, and recommends coercion if no progress occurs within a reasonable time.

1974   The Quebec government limits access to English schools to those who already have a working knowledge of English, and establishes programs for the francization of firms doing business with the government (Bill 22).

1976   Election of the Parti Québécois.

1977   The Quebec government's Bill 101 severely restricts access to English schools, directs newly arrived immigrants to French ones, introduces francization programs for all firms with more than 100 employees, and forces elimination of most English public signs. It also makes French the sole official language of the National Assembly and the courts.

1979   The Supreme Court rules that Manitoba's abrogation in 1890 of the official status of French was unconstitutional. It also declares unconstitutional the provisions of Quebec's Bill 101 that made French the sole official language of the legislature and courts.

Demographic Tables

The fourteen tables which follow are designed to give statistical information on the English and French communities of Quebec. Tables 1 to 6 describe the population in terms of mother tongue, language of general use, and ethnic origin for the province as well as for the Island of Montreal. Tables 7 to 14 focus upon the labour force and describe the differences between francophones and non-francophones in bilingualism, education, professional status, and income. With the exception of table 7, which comes from the Gendron Commission report, all the labour-force tables come from a special study commissioned by the Office de la langue française in 1979 entitled *L'Evolution de la situation socio-économique des francophones et des non-francophones au Québec (1971-1978)*.

During the 1971-1978 period, as one can see from tables 8 and 9, the percentage of English mother tongue workers in the labour force decreased while the percentage of French increased. However, the English language retained its position, because ethnic groups chose English over French. Table 10 shows that in education the over-all gap between francophones and non-francophones is gradually narrowing, but more gains are being made by women than by men. At the university level, however, the gap remained wide. It dropped from 15.4 per cent to 12.8 per cent for men and widened for women from 8.8 per cent to 13.3 per cent.

Tables 11 and 12 show that the professional and socio-economic status of francophones also improved. In 1971 the gap between francophones and non-francophones was 17 per cent and in 1978 it was 14 per cent. As far as income is concerned, francophones, particularly men, saw their incomes rise more rapidly than non-francophones from 1971 to 1978. Nevertheless, as tables 13 and 14 show, the gap remained wide. For men it went from 28.1 per cent to 19.1 per cent; for women it stayed about 12 per cent.

TABLE 1

Composition of the Population of Quebec, by Ethnic Origin and by Mother Tongue, Census Years 1851-1976

Census Year	Ethnic Origin		
	French	*British*	*Other*
1851	669,887 (75.2)[a]	215,034	5,340
1871	929,817 (78.0)	243,041	18,658
1901	1,322,115 (80.2)	290,169	36,614
1931	2,270,059 (79.0)	432,726	171,470
1951	3,327,128 (82.0)	491,818	236,735
1971	4,759,360 (79.0)	640,045	628,360

	Mother Tongue		
	French	*English*	*Other*
1931	2,292,193 (79.7)	429,613	152,449
1941	2,717,287 (81.6)	468,996	145,599
1951	3,347,030 (82.5)	558,256	150,395
1961	4,269,689 (81.2)	697,402	292,120
1971	4,867,250 (80.7)	789,185	371,330
1976	5,060,000 (81.2)	797,000	378,000

	Home Language		
	French	*English*	*Other*
1971	4,870,100 (80.8)	887,875	269,790

[a]Percentages.

Sources: Government of Canada, *1871 Census of Canada*, vol. 1 (Ottawa: Department of Agriculture, 1873), table III; Statistics Canada, 1971 Census of Canada, *Population: Ethnic Groups by Age Groups*, catalogue 92-731, bulletin 1.4-3 (Ottawa: Information Canada, 1974), table 5.

TABLE 2

Composition of the
Non-French Population of Quebec,
1871 and 1971

Ethnic origin	1871		1971	
	Number	% of population	Number	% of population
English	69,622	5.9	389,790	6.5
Scottish	49,458	4.2	108,085	1.8
Irish	123,478	10.3	139,100	2.3
Italian	n/a	—	169,655	2.8
Jewish	549	—	115,990	1.9
All others	18,109	1.6	342,725	5.7

Sources: Government of Canada, *1871 Census of Canada*, vol. 1 (Ottawa: Department of Agriculture, 1873), table III; Statistics Canada, 1971 Census of Canada, *Population: Ethnic Groups by Age Groups*, catalogue 92-731, bulletin 1.4-3 (Ottawa: Information Canada, 1974), table 5.

See Richard Joy, *Canada's Official-Language Minorities* (Montreal: C. D. Howe Research Institute, 1978), p. 25.

TABLE 3

Population by Ethnic Group: Quebec, 1971

Population	6,027,765		
British Isles	640,045	Latvian	1,415
French	4,759,360	Lithuanian	3,990
Austrian, n.o.s.	2,500	Native Indian	32,835
Belgian	8,220	Negro	5,225
Byelorussian	195	Netherlander	12,590
Chinese	11,905	Norwegian	3,820
Czech	4,420	Polish	23,970
Danish	2,630	Portuguese	16,555
East Indian	6,510	Roumanian	2,320
Indo Pakistani	5,000	Russian	4,060
Other	1,510	Slovak	2,305
Eskimo	3,755	Spanish	10,825
Estonian	1,440	Swedish	2,005
Finnish	1,865	Syrian-Lebanese	8,235
German	53,870	Ukrainian	20,325
Greek	42,870	West Indian	5,050
Hungarian	12,570	Yugoslav	6,810
Icelandic	365	Croatian	1,100
Italian	169,655	Serbian	335
Japanese	1,745	Slovenian	425
Jewish	115,990	Yugoslav, n.o.s.	4,950
		Other and unknown	25,510

Source: Census of Canada, 1971, vol 1, part 3. Immigration and Population Statistics, *Canada Immigration and Population Study* (Ottawa: Information Canada, 1974).

TABLE 4

Ethnic Composition of the Population of the Island of Montreal, 1971

French	1,155,615	59.0%
British	333,405	17.0%
Italian	148,720	7.6%
German	26,820	1.4%
Asian	32,740	1.7%
Polish	17,340	0.9%
Ukrainian	15,585	0.8%
Hungarian	9,250	0.5%
Others	219,705	11.2%
Total	1,959,180	100.0%

Source: Statistics Canada, catalogue 95-734 (CT-48).

TABLE 5

Distribution of the Population of the Island of Montreal by Mother Tongue, 1971

French	1,198,205	61.2%
English	464,775	23.7%
Others	296,165	15.1%
Total	1,959,145	100.0%

Source: Statistics Canada, catalogue 95-704 (CT-4A).

TABLE 6

Distribution of the Population of the Island of Montreal According to Language of Use, 1971

French	1,199,230	61.2%
English	537,455	27.4%
Italian	103,330	5.3%
German	8,010	0.4%
Polish	7,795	0.4%
Ukrainian	7,230	0.4%
Other	96,130	4.9%
Total	1,959,180	100.0%

Source: Statistics Canada, catalogue 95-734 (CT-4B).

TABLE 7

Bilingualism in the Labour Market, Quebec 1971

Percentage of the language groups using one or other of the language
formulas in communication at work, for the whole of Quebec

| Language groups | Language formulas | | | | TOTAL |
	Almost exclusively French	Almost exclusively English	Both languages	Other languages	
French-speaking	64% 1,165,000	3% 55,000	32% 582,000	1% 18,000	100% 1,820,000
English-speaking	5% 17,000	63% 216,000	32% 111,000	0% 	100% 344,000
Others	14% 25,000	36% 63,000	40% 71,000	10% 18,000	100% 177,000
Number of workers who use each of the formulas	1,207,000	338,000	760,000	36,000	2,341,000

Source: Survey done by the Commission of Inquiry on the Position of the French Language and on Language Rights in Quebec, *Language of Work* (Quebec: Editeur officiel du Québec, 1972), p. 17.

TABLE 8

Labour Market:
Distribution by Mother Tongue,
Montreal Region, 1971 and 1978

Mother	Percentage		Number	
tongue	*1971*	*1978*	*1971*	*1978*
French	64.3	67.0	582,700	649,031
English	22.5	19.6	203,900	189,865
Others	13.2	13.4	119,600	129,806
TOTAL	100	100	906,300	968,703

Source: Paul Bernard et al., *L'Evolution de la situation socio-économique des francophones et des non-francophones au Québec (1971-1978)* (Quebec: Editeur officiel du Québec, 1979), p. 43.

TABLE 9

Labour Market:
Linguistic Transfers, Montreal Region,
1971 and 1978

1971 (Census)

Mother tongue	Language of Use			
	French	*English*	*Others*	*TOTAL*
French	95.9%	3.9%	0.1%	100.0% 64.3%
English	5.2%	94.0%	0.8%	100.0% 22.5%
Others	8.6%	28.4%	63.0%	100.0% 13.2%
TOTAL	64.0%	27.4%	8.6%	100.0%

*1978 (IFAQ)**

Mother tongue	Language of Use			
	French	*English*	*Others*	*TOTAL*
French	96.7%	3.3%	0.0%	100.0% 67.0%
English	6.1%	93.6%	0.4%	100.0% 19.6%
Others	18.2%	48.4%	33.4%	100.0% 13.4%
TOTAL	68.4%	27.0%	4.6%	100.0%

* Survey: "Inégalités entre francophones et anglophones au Québec" (IFAQ).
Source: Paul Bernard et al., p. 68.

TABLE 10

Labour Market:
Distribution of Francophones and Non-francophones
According to Their Level of Education, by Sex, 1971 and 1978

Level of education	UFMTQ* 1971						IFAQ 1978					
	Men		Women		Total		Men		Women		Total	
	F	NF	F	NF	F	NF	F	NF	F	NF	F	NF
0-7 years	30.3	16.3	16.8	13.1	26.2	15.5	20.5	12.9	10.3	8.4	17.1	11.3
8-10 years	29.8	25.2	27.4	16.0	29.1	22.4	25.1	15.9	18.6	10.3	22.9	14.1
11-12 years												
College without diploma	25.6	30.5	38.4	47.8	29.5	35.5	35.1	41.4	45.9	46.7	38.7	43.2
College with diploma	6.0	4.3	12.1	9.1	7.9	5.7	7.5	5.3	18.1	13.9	11.1	8.1
University	8.2	23.6	5.1	13.9	7.3	20.8	11.8	24.6	7.2	20.5	10.2	23.4
TOTAL	100%	100%	100%	100%	100%	100%	100%	100%	100%	100%	100%	100%

* Survey done by the Centre de sondage de l'Université de Montréal for the Gendron Commission called "L'Utilisation du français dans le monde du travail du Québec" (UFMTQ).
Source: Paul Bernard et al., p. 98.

TABLE 11
Labour Market: Distribution of Francophones and Non-francophones by Occupation and by Sex, 1971 and 1978

Sectors	UFMTQ 1971						IFAQ 1978					
	Men		Women		Total		Men		Women		Total	
	F	NF	F	NF	F	NF	F	NF	F	NF	F	NF
— Managerial, administrative, and related occupations	10.0	17.4	4.3	4.5	8.2	13.6	9.2	16.6	3.4	4.1	7.3	12.5
— Natural sciences, engineering, mathematics	2.3	7.1	0.7	1.2	1.8	5.3	4.0	7.3	0.3	2.6	2.8	5.8
— Social sciences and related fields	1.4	1.4	2.3	1.6	1.7	1.5	1.4	1.7	1.0	1.5	1.3	1.6
— Teaching and related occupations	3.1	3.4	9.8	11.1	5.2	5.7	3.7	3.9	10.3	10.4	5.9	6.1
— Medicine and health	2.4	1.8	10.7	8.0	4.9	3.6	1.9	1.7	10.2	10.2	4.7	4.5
— Artistic, literary, recreational, and related occupations	1.5	2.4	2.1	1.6	1.7	2.2	1.7	3.5	1.1	3.0	1.5	3.3
— Clerical and related occupations	8.0	9.6	27.2	41.9	14.0	19.2	7.4	10.4	39.9	43.0	18.3	21.0
— Sales	10.0	9.9	8.2	6.4	9.4	8.9	10.7	11.1	5.6	8.9	9.0	10.4
— Service	11.0	6.4	14.9	7.6	12.3	6.8	8.4	5.8	12.6	6.5	9.9	6.0
— Farming, horticultural, and animal husbandry	5.3	1.3	1.5	0.5	4.1	1.1	3.5	1.8	0.3	1.0	2.4	1.5
— Fishing, hunting, trapping, and related occupations	3.2	0.6	0.1	0.0	2.3	0.4	2.1	0.2	0.0	0.0	1.4	0.1
— Processing occupations	8.0	5.0	3.7	1.7	6.6	4.0	5.9	3.7	1.5	0.1	4.5	2.5
— Machining and related, product fabricating, assembling and repairing	14.9	17.0	11.9	12.0	14.0	15.5	15.9	16.8	11.5	7.3	14.4	13.6
— Construction trades	7.3	5.5	0.3	0.0	5.2	3.8	12.0	7.1	0.0	0.0	8.0	4.8
— Transport	7.1	7.6	0.4	0.2	5.0	5.4	6.6	4.1	0.2	0.0	4.5	2.8
— Other occupations	4.7	3.6	2.0	1.5	3.8	3.0	5.3	4.5	2.0	1.3	4.2	3.4
TOTAL	100%	100%	100%	100%	100%	100%	100%	100%	100%	100%	100%	100%

Source: Paul Bernard et al., p. 116.

TABLE 12

Labour Market: Occupations: Coefficients of Dissimilarities between Francophones and Non-francophones by Two Classifications, by Sex and by Year

	1971			1978		
	Men	*Women*	*Total*	*Men*	*Women*	*Total*
By type of activity	17.8	16.9	17.2	17.0	12.5	14.7
By socio-economic status	18.5	15.1	17.4	17.1	10.8	14.3

Source: Paul Bernard et al., p. 99.

TABLE 13

Labour Market: Distribution of Francophones and Non-francophones According to Income Level, by Sex, 1971 and 1978

	Census 1971						IFAQ 1978					
	Men		Women		Total		Men		Women		Total	
Annual income before deductions	F	NF	F	NF	F	NF	F	NF	F	NF	F	NF
less than $7,500	32.1	25.1	66.2	60.2	42.3	36.0	22.1	16.9	48.9	39.0	31.2	24.0
$7,500—$10,499	22.9	17.1	20.3	23.7	22.2	19.2	14.2	12.7	22.9	27.6	17.1	17.4
$10,500—$13,499	20.0	18.5	8.2	9.4	16.7	15.6	20.3	17.0	16.5	19.0	19.0	17.6
$13,500—$16,499	10.5	10.4	3.2	3.1	8.3	8.2	15.1	11.2	5.7	8.4	11.9	10.2
$16,500—$19,499	6.1	9.0	1.3	1.7	4.7	6.8	11.6	13.3	3.9	3.7	9.1	10.3
$19,500 or more	8.2	19.7	0.8	1.9	6.1	14.2	16.9	28.8	2.0	2.3	11.9	20.3
TOTAL	100%	100%	100%	100%	100%	100%	100%	100%	100%	100%	100%	100%

Source: Paul Bernard et al., p. 126.